The story of Illawalla, an extraordinary house near Blackpool, the people who lived there, and the tragedies that affected them.

For Christine Orme, with grateful thanks.

© David Richard Taylor, October 2020

Beloved Ghosts

PREAMBLE	3
CHAPTER 1. VISIT TO GUILDFORD – 2005	4
CHAPTER 2. CONVERSATION WITH FATHER – 1	8
CHAPTER 3. EARLY CHILDHOOD – 1939-1945	9
CHAPTER 4. DAVID'S ACCIDENT – 1962	11
CHAPTER 5. CHEW MAGNA, 1841	13
CHAPTER 6. ILLAWALLA, THE HOUSE	20
CHAPTER 7. ILLAWALLA, THE CONTINUING STORY	22
CHAPTER 8. LIVING AT ILLAWALLA	24
CHAPTER 9. THE START TO MY LEGAL CAREER	26
CHAPTER 10. FATHER	28
CHAPTER 11. MY SISTER VALERIE – 1964	32
CHAPTER 12. A TERRIBLE INCIDENT – 1985	46
CHAPTER 13. DOROTHY – 1988	53
CHAPTER 14. MARILYN'S DISAPPEARANCE – 2001	55
CHAPTER 15. ANOTHER MEETING WITH FATHER – 2	57
CHAPTER 16. TRICIA AND HER TRIP TO BRAZIL	58
CHAPTER 17. EPILOGUE	63
CHAPTER 18. FINAL MEETING WITH FATHER – 3	65

PREAMBLE

We all live in a cocoon of memory. Do you remember the time when? What does that particular song bring back? Someone saying something? A perfume? A noise? A summer's day? But most of all a song, because it best conjures up the time, the place or the person. A song not only can, but will, transport you, and then one can smile, laugh or cry in that strange enchanted land of memory, or the uncharted land of regret.

David (my friend) would be any Johnny Mathis song, as we listened to him the night before the accident. My sister Valerie would be anything by Dickie Valentine. My vanished sister Marilyn would be anything from Annie Get Your Gun. My father would be Begin the Beguine. My dear Aunt Amy would be the Merry Widow Waltz. My grandfather would be the Soldiers of the Queen (his Queen would have been Victoria). Some characters have no songs. Funny that. Others will appear and disappear in this maelstrom of memories.

We all live in the past and try to imagine the future.

"My theme is memory, that winged host, that soared about me one grey morning of war-time. These memories which are my life - for we possess nothing certainly except the past - were always with me"

"I return link by link along the iron chains of memory"

Lawrence Durrell, like Evelyn Waugh, came to me later in life. I recognised them instantly when they appeared. Soulmates!

"The life that is lived wholly in memory is the most perfect conceivable. The satisfactions of memory are richer than reality and have a security no reality possesses." – Kierkegaard

This book is written from memory, for my loved ones.

This is a story of five deaths, a missing person, an extraordinary person living in an extraordinary house, and a broken man, all interlinked by a common denominator – me.

My Latin teacher told me 'haec olim meminisse iuvabit'... One day this will be pleasing to remember. I wonder.

This book draws no conclusions, nor attempts to offer explanations where explanations are not possible.

It is a story of my beloved ghosts.

Beloved Ghosts

CHAPTER 1. VISIT TO GUILDFORD – 2005

I had come to Guildford to see some old friends. They were friends from my student and rugby days at Guildford, and I was looking forward to seeing them.

I had booked into a hotel in the town centre, and was ambling up the High Street having had breakfast, not going anywhere in particular, but just reliving old memories.

I know it sounds dramatic, but I suddenly felt an urge, or imagined I heard a voice saying "Go, now! Go and see them!"

I did as I was told, paid my hotel bill, got the car out of the car park, and drove in the direction of my friends' house, although I did not know exactly how to get there.

When I got near, I pulled over to the side of the road, half on the pavement, to look at my street map.

Suddenly, there was a loud sound of a car horn, and I looked to see a lady driver in the middle of the road gesticulating at me, to say that I had parked across her driveway. I waved my hand in acknowledgement, mouthed "sorry", and drew the car forward to continue reading my map.

The next thing, there was a knock on the window. I wound the window down, and saw it was the lady from the car.

She apologised for gesticulating so aggressively at me, and, of course, I said "It doesn't matter. It was my fault. I am very sorry". She then asked where I was going, and I explained. She knew the area, and was able to direct me.

She then said "Would you like to come in for a coffee?"

I felt that I had to speak to this lady. I felt *compelled* to speak to this lady.

I walked up her path, following her. She and I were welcomed by her dogs, who seemed to have free run of the place. She asked me to sit down, and offered me the drink she had previously promised. I had a coffee.

We sat talking generalities, but I told her nothing of myself except my Christian name, that I had been a law student in Guildford, and was here to see friends. She, in turn, told me her name was J__, and that she had lived in Guildford for many years with her husband. Our conversation of general polite chatter continued.

Every so often, she would stand up and go upstairs, and I would hear voices. Clearly she was speaking to herself, but as if another person were present with her. Each time she came downstairs, she was in an increasingly agitated state.

On the last occasion she came down, she looked really quite upset, and was holding her head in her hands. She pointed at me, and said "It's you isn't it? It's you. I knew I had to see you, they want to talk to you. They have been at me all morning. My head! My head!"

Of course, by this time, I was getting quite concerned, although clearly the lady was no physical threat to me, and was genuinely upset.

Just to pause for a second, one must think of the amazing coincidence of my journey, coming from Guildford High Street, at a random moment, to park across this lady's driveway at exactly the time she returned from shopping, having come back by a different way (she told me this later) from her usual route. A few seconds either way, and we would have missed each other.

Please believe me that in telling this story, I have nothing to gain by lying or exaggerating. Whichever way I tell it, it does not put me in a better or worse light. J__ gained nothing from the encounter either i.e. no money was asked for or given, though I did send her some flowers.

So it began, something which has never left me, and something I do not understand.

I cast my mind back to the conversation we had, in order to be sure that I gave her no clue as to my identity.

She stood up again, pacing the room holding her head, "They want to speak to you. They have to speak to you. They are here for you. The room is filled with them."

She slumped in her chair, holding her head. I asked her whether I could get her a glass of water or help her in any way. She shook her head and said "I see lots of people, some happy, some sad, some in pain, some angry."

I have a good recall of all this because of my lawyers training, and the fact that she allowed me to take

Beloved Ghosts

notes, which I still have.

"What do you see?" I asked.

"A lady. Short dark hair. Nice smile. She has gone over by her own hand. She is smiling and talking. I can't really tell what she's saying... oh yes, she is saying 'Dave'?"

And then to me, she asked "Who called you Dave?"

Well, I had told her my name was David, so that was not particularly brilliant.

However, my sister Marilyn had called me Dave, the only one in the family to do so, but so far as I was aware she was still alive, although I had not seen her for years, and I believed she was somewhere in Europe.

"My sister Marilyn called me Dave, but as far as I know she is alive"

"Well, she has gone over." J__ said, "She didn't bother to save herself".

And then she said "Oh! What an angry man! He's shouting and pointing at the dark haired girl. He has a message for you. He says 'She is your kith and kin. Do something about it – sort it out!'"

She described the man in detail. Clearly this was my father. Wherever he was, he was just as angry and bitter as he had been in life. I was still scared of him.

"Who else do you see?"

"I see an old man. He has a nice aura. He's short, old, with a walking stick, dressed in a three-piece suit, wearing a trilby. He's gesturing with his stick and pointing." Clearly, this was my grandfather.

She said "I see a big garden. I see horses, dogs, and a big house. I see cattle in the bottom field. Oh, lovely, lovely - what a lovely man!" She was clearly near to tears.

She then told me of all the people that were there. In fact, she paraded most of my family that day.

She described my sister Valerie, and said "Oh, the poor girls' face!"

She described Dorothy, "Such a gentle person, so ill when she passed. She sends her love to you"

By this time, of course, I was getting to be more agitated. But the lawyer in me kicked in, and I tried to ask what I thought were incisive questions. I asked "Why can I not speak to them?" to which J__ replied:

"They only speak through me, although you can ask any questions you want."

"Please ask my mother if she has forgiven father."

Mother's reply came back in the form of a question to me "Have YOU forgiven father? I can. Can you? You must forgive him immediately. You must say thirty-five times a day, for seven days 'I forgive my father completely'"

"Why has nobody given their names or identified themselves?"

J__ replied "To make you believe. Do you remember when you went to the Spiritualist Centre in London? You went twice, didn't you? On each occasion, your guide gave you names – any number of names. And not one of them meant anything to you. Believe in the people. The names are not important."

It was true. I had gone twice to the Spiritualist Centre, but had not mentioned this to her.

I asked "Why are they here?"

She answered "They have come to comfort you. You have given so much to life, and had so much taken from you. They said 'we want to help this man, because he is lost.' They wish to end your turmoil. You have thrashed around all your life. They want you to fulfil your ambition, to be a kind and loving human being. They wish to pour balm on you." All the wording sounded strange to me.

I then said "Where are these people now?"

She replied "They are on an intermediate plane, waiting for you to take them up, because they can only ascend with you. But in time - they are happy, and you will not die young."

She made other points at random, and to try and demonstrate the veracity of what she was saying: she described my sister Valerie as having "crinkly hair", which she did: She told me some of the breeds and names of the dogs that we used to have. She told me how I used to live with Dorothy in a small bedroom, and she described Dorothy's laugh.

There was, of course, much more. They were all minute details, reminders of days and times gone by, but they did much to convince me of the truth.

The séance or session finished as quickly as it began, and we both sat there equally drained. I would guess the whole episode lasted between one to two hours, and I felt more than strange – completely disconnected from my body.

J__ said, "When you get home, spray your house to get rid of all your 'travails'. Again, an odd word, and not a word I would normally use.

I made to leave, and took a note of her name and address, which she gave me willingly. As I said, she did not ask for money, and I did not offer or give any. As I was getting into the car, she said "Be very careful when you switch on the engine. You will still be full of their spirit."

I got in the car, and turned on the ignition. There was a loud explosion, and smoke from the engine. The battery appeared to be dead, and the engine would not turn.

She said "I did warn you. You'll have to ring the AA. Come in and have another coffee while you wait for them."

So back inside to a different type of story, and mystery.

We went back into the house, phoned the AA and had another coffee. She was now more relaxed, and happy to talk. She had always had the "gift" as she called it. She also called it a curse. She had never been a professional medium as such, but had performed on stage on occasions.

Her friends and family knew of her abilities, and they frequently asked her to try and make contact. She tried to emphasise that the spirits came to her, rather than the other way around.

Very often, she did make contact, but pretended she had not. On one occasion, she was asked by a friend of the family to prepare a life chart for her friend's two sons. She started the task, but had to abandon it, as she could see one of the boys would die at 16 years old in a motorcycle accident. The friend sensed something was wrong, but J__ could do nothing. The terrible event duly occurred. I asked her why she could not say anything- and she replied that "it was written, and I could not change what was pre-ordained".

I said "Why not keep the boy off the bike for a year, or lock him in his room?" to which she said "It would have happened anyway, somehow."

She said that on several occasions, she had been able to see into the future, but always tried to say nothing negative, or hurtful, to anyone.

Then she gave me a funny look and said "Your wife is very ill, isn't she?"

I had, of course, never mentioned that I was married. I told her that she was right, and then asked whether Tricia would survive.

She asked if I really wanted to know. I said I did, because I had a bad feeling anyway.

J__ said "She will pass early next year."

Tricia died in April 2006.

She also said "You live in the country, don't you? Well, be careful when you get home- you will have a slight car crash, but no one will be hurt".

Within two days of getting home, I had ploughed my car into a gate post. There is no reason for me to do so. I was not going fast, and road conditions were good. I looked at the skid marks after the accident, and it was as if the car had been moved sideways. I did not, and still do not, understand why I had that collision.

She said "You have had a lot of tragedies, and you will suffer again". I assume she meant that something would happen to Tricia, so I did not press that issue.

The AA man arrived. I explained what had happened. He lifted the bonnet, but could not see any problem. He turned the ignition key, and the car started first time and ran smoothly. I asked him if he could see if there had been anything wrong. In reply, he said he said he did not understand why he had been called out.

Just as I was leaving, J__ said "I have to tell someone about all this, because it has been quite a morning for me, too. Do you know there is only one person I could tell, and that's my friend who lives nearby, at No. 2 ___ Road?"

As she said this, she looked directly at me as if to get a reaction. She got one. No. 2 ___ Road was where my first wife, Annie, had been living when I met her in 1962, 43 years previously!

I left J__, and went to see the people I intended to visit in the first place. The door to the house was open and Tony, my friend, was standing there. He said "Where have you been? We have been waiting for you."

Beloved Ghosts

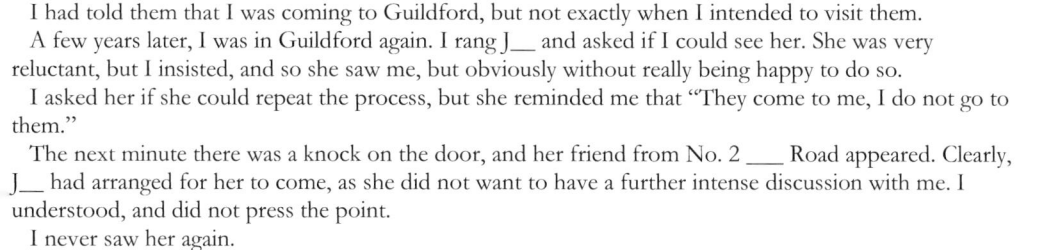

I had told them that I was coming to Guildford, but not exactly when I intended to visit them.

A few years later, I was in Guildford again. I rang J__ and asked if I could see her. She was very reluctant, but I insisted, and so she saw me, but obviously without really being happy to do so.

I asked her if she could repeat the process, but she reminded me that "They come to me, I do not go to them."

The next minute there was a knock on the door, and her friend from No. 2 ___ Road appeared. Clearly, J__ had arranged for her to come, as she did not want to have a further intense discussion with me. I understood, and did not press the point.

I never saw her again.

CHAPTER 2. CONVERSATION WITH FATHER – 1

I had a long conversation with my father after he had died. I say long, but in reality it was only a few minutes, but that was long for him – and for me.

He was walking along the promenade. He walked in his usual fashion, half limping (arthritis), but trying to hurry, as if he had somewhere to go. Which of course, he didn't, because he was dead.

He tried to pretend he had not seen me, but he could not avoid me, as I stood directly in his path. He faced me, but sideways on, not quite facing me, avoiding my eyes, pretending he was pleased to see me.

"How are you?" Either of us could have said that, but I think it was me.

"Alright"

"What's it like then?"

"What?"

"Where you are"

Well that started it. He did not like the place, he did not like the food. Worst of all, he did not like the people. He was pretty much as I expected him to be. Never in his life was he ever grateful or happy with anything. Occasionally, he pretended to be grateful, like when grandfather bought a house for him and mother, but generally gratitude was replaced with simmering resentment.

He always maintained he could get along without help from anybody. He was a capable man, capable of doing a job, a master printer, not much of a drinker, a brilliant impromptu pianist, who could play pretty much anything, and who had his own trio for dancing at the age of 16. That was before the war, of course.

Anyway, back to the conversation. "Have you thought any more about what you did?" I asked.

No reply from him, as he turned his back on me and walked away.

I shrugged. I did not care. We would meet again, and we would not have a conversation again.

It was interesting how many souls paraded along that promenade. In their 20's and from the Twenties, in their youth, in their adolescence, and in their senility.

We were all in another place, although I am not quite sure where.

CHAPTER 3. EARLY CHILDHOOD – 1939-1945

At last I can start this thing, this story that has bugged me all my life, and has taken me until I am 80 years old, to suddenly realise that I can do this. Unfortunately in life, work intervenes to prevent you doing something that you want. Anyway, so long as one acts within the constraints of decency to others, one can pretty much say anything.

What a life it has been, so many deaths, a rollicking rollercoaster of a life, as the dust jacket might have it. So much fun, so many people wandering in and out of my life, each making their marks and memories - some leaving pain, but most leaving a smile on my lips, as I remember their kindness or their silliness, or their laughter.

Before I tell you about throwing myself into the arms of an almost complete stranger in late 1945, let me put into the pot a few random memories of the war years. Here are the photographs. Look at them carefully. Look at their wartime faces. Imagine their thoughts and fears. Of course, I was too young, at the time but I now realise the significance of those photographs.

Mother's brother, Ronnie, smiling shortly before being posted to Singapore, and his death as a prisoner of war, in a ship sunk by the Japanese. There's mother's other brother, Gordon. He survived the war in the RAF, but died of prostate cancer years later. There's Mary, father's sister. In one of her letters she wrote "I am dying to have a crack at the Boche" and "that man Hitler just dished my holidays". Yes, she really did say those things- almost a parody of a true blue English lady! Capture the flavour of times past, and look through their masks to the worries and anxieties of their time.

Of course, I can only tell you what I know from my personal experiences of their lives, as I have not researched their lives in any great detail. The facts will be wrapped in myths, and the myths will be wrapped in the memories of a young boy growing into manhood, trying to get to grips with life, and with the impressions of his elders tainted to no little extent by family rivalry, disparity of income, and differences of background.

I was born just before the outbreak of war. My birth did not cause hostilities. It was an unnoticed event, except by my family.

So what about the war? I can remember the sounds of bombs, but slept soundly in my cot in the cellar of the family home called Beech House, somewhere in Salford.

Eventually, because of the incessant bombing, we had to leave, and went to live on the Fylde Coast at Cleveleys.

My grandfather was an important man, an MP (Member of Parliament, not Military Policeman), and he spent most of his time in London.

My father, that dead man from the Guildford experience and the walk on the promenade, had volunteered just before hostilities broke out, so I spent the first six years of my life not knowing about men.

The occupants of the semi-detached house on the promenade at Cleveleys were my mother, her mother, my dear Aunt Amy – and me, cosseted, loved, and incapable of doing any wrong.

I can recall standing at the top of the stairs in the house in Cleveleys listening to the three ladies deciding what to do if a German paratrooper knocked at the door. Would they offer him a cup of tea? That must have been near the end of the war, as I kind of understood what they were talking about.

I remember my father coming home on leave, and sharing my bed. However, I felt him get out at night to make nocturnal visits to my mother. Why didn't he start with her at the beginning of the night? Even in the 1940's, husbands and wives were permitted to sleep together. Clearly a foreshadowing of the terrible end to my parents' marriage.

I have visualised myself leaping down the whole flight of stairs to land triumphantly at the bottom. I remember a toy garage with one tiny, battery operated bulb. I remember a wooden toy monkey climbing up a stick. I remember a Mr. Bull, who had something to do with a black market, although I could not imagine what a black market was. I remember the indescribable delight, one Christmas, of being given a kaleidoscope. I remember my Aunt Amy singing to me (she was known as the "Wigan Nightingale"... what a picture that phrase conjures up). She sang light opera. To hear the Merry Widow Waltz even now takes me back to that kind lady, who always read to me, and told me about the pre-war Blackpool

Beloved Ghosts

Illuminations, and, more important, always had time for me.

She gave me my first interest in movies, long before I realised it was the family business. She loved Fred Astaire. She told me the stories of the various movies, and that was how I learned about Beau Geste, Wuthering Heights and Random Harvest, long before I read the books.

More important, she brought the books to life for me, by giving me descriptions of the main characters.

I remember my grandfather, the MP making occasional visits from London. He was to play a big part in my later life, but in Cleveleys, he was only a bit player, like my father, an occasional visitor to a house dominated by women.

I cannot remember what I read in those late wartime days. I would certainly have read something, as my mother was RADA trained, keen on the classics. She gave me a love of books and words, and of course, a certain sentimentality in anything I recited. I can remember reciting, but cannot remember reading or learning "Driver Jim" and "The Green Eye of the Little Yellow God". I am told that I brought tears to the eyes of my doting aunts and their friends (no uncles, no men, all away fighting, or on war work, except Mr. Bull, who was tending his black market).

So I spent my first few years surrounded by loving ladies, little or no discipline, in a happy kind environment. A place and time to look back on through blurred eyes, a warm memory, so rudely to be shattered by a demobbed FATHER.

Apparently I was cultured and intelligent! I was perfect... and spoiled. So that when father came back from the war, he was determined to de-spoil his brat of a son, and that started a lifelong animosity between the two of us.

He started off by imbuing in me a sense of worthlessness, which has never left me, and which I will take to my grave.

He once said that I was too nice. He said it sneeringly as an insult.

I can imagine him saying "What are you doing writing a book? Do not mention me." Oh no? But he always wanted to be the centre of attention whenever he played the piano.

What a complex, damaged, unhappy man, who managed to make many of the people close to him unhappy as well, although his friends never knew that.

Beloved Ghosts

CHAPTER 4. DAVID'S ACCIDENT – 1962

In 1961, I went to Guildford. I was there to study for my Law examinations, and I went into digs on the Epsom Road.

The landlord was an ex-naval Commander, who ran the house as he must have run his ship.

There were six of us, all in our early twenties, young lads on the threshold of whatever life had to offer.

Eric became a County Court judge, and had a distinguished career in the law.

In 2007, he left his chambers to drive home and was caught in a torrential flood. The car stalled, the waters rose, and he was talking to his wife on the phone as he drowned.

In our days, in Guildford, he was the happiest soul, and the nicest man. We were good friends.

Every afternoon, he and I would walk down the road to a local cafe, and there, over tea and toast, we would test each other's knowledge of the law, in preparation for our forthcoming exams.

I can still see that tea room in my memory, some sixty years on.

Robert was the dour and reticent type. He had worked in industry, funnily enough in a company of which my grandfather had been a Director. He loved Majorca. I lost track of him at the end of our course, never to hear from him again.

Dai, obviously Welsh, passionate and fiery. However, one day he destroyed his credibility with us by letting his anti-Jewish feelings be known. This was unfortunate, because two of the other students, George and Paul, were in fact, Jewish, and there was an embarrassed silence at lunch when Dai set off on his rant. He apologised, but the damage was done.

David was from Liverpool, and we became firm friends because of our Northern connections, and the fact that we both played rugby.

So there we have the cast, but only two of us were the main players in the events which were to follow.

David and I joined the local rugby club Guildford and Godalming, where the standard of play was not particularly high, but the enjoyment, particularly post match, was top level.

On the 3rd February 1962, we were due to play against local rivals, Horsham.

David had been given a brand new Austin Healey Sprite by his family, and we decided that we would travel in that car to play at Horsham.

The night before, we went into Guildford Town Centre, a short walk from the digs, where we behaved as lads did at that age and in that time – we had a drink or two and a polite chat with two girls we sort of knew. Remember it was the early 60's, and we were all much gentler then, less sure of ourselves.

The girls kindly invited us back to their flat for coffee, and we listened to Johnny Mathis (how innocent we all were). So, his music will forever more conjure up an image of David for me. Such a moving thought.

It is impossible to look back on that evening, without thinking of the tragedy that was to unfold just a few hours ahead.

Anyway, the following day, we drove to Horsham, and played our game of rugby.

In those distant days, the BBC used to read out the rugby results, and so I said to David, and I will regret this for the rest of my life, "Let's listen to the results on the car radio, and then drive back to Guildford for a night out".

We had no time for a drink. We listened to the results, and set off on the short journey back to Guildford.

There we were, in the prime of our lives, at the beginning of the 60's and our careers, and, in effect our lives, singing along to whatever was on the radio and looking forward to our night out. Moon River was one of the hit songs of the moment.

The opposite traffic flow was very heavy, as it was the main road to Brighton, and people were heading there for the weekend.

So, driving along steadily, singing – happy – David, suddenly, without warning or signal, took a very sharp turn to the left, off the main road, down a farm track. He stopped immediately, and I said to him "Why did you do that? Why did you turn off?"

He said "Don't know. Haven't a clue."

We used Rugby players language to each other.

He carefully reversed his car and re-joined the traffic flow. We were on that farm track about a minute.

Driving along, I remember all the headlights of the cars going the opposite way, and, then in a split second, I saw the headlights of a car on the wrong side of the road. After that, blackness.

I next found myself standing outside a huge door. It was like the castle door out of the Robin Hood film starring Errol Flynn. From within came the sound of music and laughter, as if a great party were in progress. I had the feeling that I just had to open that door, and I would step into happiness.

I hammered on the door and desperately tried to open it.

The urge was strong, but hands were preventing me.

I came to, and the hands I had felt were from a complete stranger, who was dragging me out of what had been David's car. I lay on the roadside with headlights shining, engines running, and people rushing to and fro. Next, I heard sirens, and I was lifted and placed into an ambulance. I could feel moisture on my face, which I assumed to be blood, and I could see that my right knee was bleeding profusely.

The ambulance door opened, and a man who said he was a doctor examined me, saying "You'll be alright, but I'm afraid that poor chap in the car has had it".

The ambulance filled gradually. Three young men I did not know were brought in, one on a stretcher and two walking. One said "I'm so sorry, it was my fault", and he then appeared to pass out. The ambulance door opened again, and a stretcher with a body was placed on the opposite side of the ambulance to me. I knew it was David, because the blanket which covered his body was not long enough, and I could see his feet and his black shiny shoes.

So to Guildford hospital, for an operation to repair all my cuts and scrapes, and to gently knit me together again. There followed a gradual realisation of what had happened.

It was clear that David had seen the oncoming headlights, and had braked as hard as possible. There were no seatbelts in those days, and the braking must have thrown me forward, so that I smashed my head on the dashboard. I was therefore unconscious and limp at the moment of impact, and that may have saved my life.

My right knee was ripped apart on the sharp shelf of the glove compartment.

David took the full impact of the steering wheel on his unprotected chest.

So why did David go down that farm track? There was no reason for him to do so. He offered no explanation. People have said that he was too early for his own death. Is that possible?

I also realise that I had a near death experience. I firmly believe that if I had gone through the door I described, I would have died. The only thing I can say to that, is that it was not a scary experience. It was warm and inviting. I felt no pain.

I have never forgotten David. He was a physically big man, very tall, and I can see him now bending to get through a doorway, as we were drinking in one of the many happy Guildford hostelries. I was going to say he would have been a friend for life. In actual fact he was... for his short life.

One last comment, for what it is worth. The young driver was charged with causing death by dangerous driving. Between the accident and his trial (at which he was found guilty) his hair had turned white.

Poor chap – to have to live with that for the rest of his life – but of course, David did not have a "rest of his life". Some sort of justice?

David's body was taken back to Liverpool for his funeral, although due to the distance and my injuries, I was unable to attend.

Later, a memorial service was arranged, to be held in Guildford Cathedral.

I was terrified at the thought of having to relive the accident, and having to console David's family and friends. I was, of course, guilty at having survived. I had more drinks than were good for me at the lunch time preceding the afternoon service. I then went back to my digs to change, fell asleep, and to my shame, missed the service.

Self defence mechanism? Another regret to add to the many of my life.

People kindly said that they understood my absence.

Beloved Ghosts

CHAPTER 5. CHEW MAGNA, 1841

How does one imagine one's ancestors?

Does one actually try and picture them in the fashion of the time? Were they tall or short? Did the men have beards? What clothes did the ladies wear? Were the ladies equal to the men? Or were they servile? There may have been some early photographs of that time, but none that can be identified as actually being my ancestors.

I would have loved to have seen them, to see whether any male characteristics had carried through the family.

People are described in the census for a particular year, for example as a blacksmith, as were two of my ancestors, or, merely as a person, without occupation, waiting to move on to allow room for the next generation.

Through successive censuses, people age before one's eyes until they are finally removed, leaving a blank space where they had formerly existed.

Looking at the names, in my case, the Emery family, I wonder what they did all day? Indeed, what were they actually doing on the day of the census? Not their jobs (if any) which were described in the censuses, but how did they pass their lives? What time did they go to work? What did they have for lunch? What did they do for leisure? How did they pass the long winter evenings? What was their 'happiness'? More mundanely, what was the weather like? Of course, it always seems to be fine in the past years of one's imagination.

So the blacksmith working in his sweltering shop would have stood outside for some fresh air, and no doubt talked and gossiped with the neighbours, some of whom he would have been related to, and some of whose families and descendants would join with his family and descendants in his or their unforeseen futures.

It is very hard to keep reminding myself that life is a comedy, as my ancestors must have had some bitter times in some bitter weather, rather than the permanent sunshine of memory.

I am looking back to 1841, and to the village of Chew Magna in Somerset, a small village with a population of a few hundred. I chose this time and place to begin the story of the journey eventually undertaken by my great great grandfather in 1881 or 1882, when he decided that there was not enough work available, so he walked from Chew Magna to Wigan to find employment in the coal mines.

However, my starting ancestor for the purposes of this book is my great great great grandfather Joshua Emery, who was born in 1796 in the midst of the Napoleonic wars. He would have heard about the battle of Trafalgar as a nine year old child, and ten years later, he would have celebrated the victory at Waterloo.

He married his wife Ann in December 1814 when he was 18. He was the village blacksmith, and he and Ann produced three children, John, George and Isaac. John, who was described as a Smith Journeyman in the 1841 census, was born in 1820.

John is the predecessor carrier of my genes so, rather brutally, we are not concerned with his brothers, George and Isaac, nor his sister Ann who came along later.

John eventually married Martha Pickford who had been born in 1822. John and Martha were prolific breeders who, in the fullness of time, would produce Emma, Martha, Henry, Charles, Amelia, William, Alfred, John, Ellen, Walter and Albert.

What did they all do? What were their histories? Their futures? Because in this snapshot of time, they all had a future. How did they all find work? Of all John's children, William, born in 1860 was the immediate forebear of mine and it is his blood that would eventually mingle with mine, and so it will be his bloodline that we are following.

In the 1881 census, William was listed as a labourer and was living at home with his father John, mother Martha and only two brothers Walter and Alfred.

Late in 1881 or early 1882, he decided that he had had enough and so choose to make the long walk North to find work.

It is 185 miles from Chew Magna to Wigan and walking at 2 or 3 miles an hour, with suitable rests, allowing for no travel at night, and dependant on the time of year, it would have taken nine or ten days actual travel to make the trek.

Beloved Ghosts

William Emery must have met Ruth Dootson soon after coming to Wigan, as they married in 1882 when he was 22, and they had already been living together at Albert Cottage, Standish, Wigan. Ruth was the landlady of a local pub, and from her photograph, she appears to be a somewhat formidable figure. Perhaps the photograph was taken later in her life.

William had made progress from his initial mining work in the pits, to becoming a Check Weighman, a job which entailed agreeing figures with the Mine Owners' Check Weighman, as miners were then paid by the weight of coal mined.

Wigan was a major mining area. There were nearly 1000 pits listed in the Wigan area in the 1880's, the first pit in the area having been opened in 1450, 35 years after the Battle of Agincourt.

William and Ruth had five children, Mary, William, Harry, Winifred and my maternal grandfather James Frederick, who was born on 17th December 1886.

The whole family lived in a one-up one-down cottage in Lower Ground Standish, Wigan. It goes without saying that they were very poor.

Fifty or so years later, my grandfather was on speaking terms with Winston Churchill, wealthy, an MP, a business owner, and a happy family man.

He put his achievements down to hard work and a great deal of luck. Most successful people will say the same.

He told me about the hardship of his childhood in Wigan. He particularly remembered that one night a goat had wandered into the village. There was no animal protection or sentiment at that time, because everyone was hungry. The goat was dispatched forthwith and roasted on an open fire for the benefit of all.

He was educated at the local school, Crook School, and the headmaster at that time, Mr. James Lyon, spotted the potential in young Fred, who sometimes used to skate to school on the canal.

He left school in 1899, aged 13. Queen Victoria was on the throne. The British Empire was at its height, ruling nearly a quarter of the globe.

Nevertheless, those were truly hard days, and most parents were happy to see their sons leave school and join their fathers and grandfathers down the pits.

Fred's headmaster, however, had faith in the young man, and he persuaded Fred's parents to let him join the Lancashire and Yorkshire Railway – and this he did, becoming a telegraphist at Gathurst Station, Wigan, in December 1899.

His working week was 72 hours, 6am to 5pm, Monday to Saturday, and 9am to 3pm Sunday, followed by an easy week of 56 hours. He still somehow found time to study, teaching himself shorthand and typing, using a cardboard imitation of a typewriter keyboard, which he had bought for a few pence.

He was then placed in the District Managers' office in Bolton in 1906, where his ever increasing thirst for knowledge led him to evening classes and examination success. The directors of the Railway Company awarded him a scholarship to Manchester University, where he studied economics under Professor Sir Sydney Chapman. This education was to serve him well in later life. He apparently passed his exams, but was unable to afford the few shillings that were required to confirm his degree, and he was never able to call himself a B. Econ.

He married Florence Beatrice Gradwell on the 15th April 1912. That was the day the Titanic sank, and grandfather used to comment, jokingly, in later life, that there were two disasters on the same day.

In July 1914, he was appointed General Manager of a group of Indian Light Railways, but his emigration to India was interrupted by the outbreak of war. Enlisting in the Lancashire Fusiliers in the early part of the war, he was almost immediately transferred back to the railway, as employment on the railways was a protected occupation, like farmers and miners. Almost certainly, his work saved his life, because the Lancashire Fusiliers were sent to Gallipoli, where the casualties were horrific.

So, in about 1916 or 1917, while still working on the railway, he being dissatisfied with his job, talked his brother Billy into hiring the local village hall and a cinema projector. They hung a sheet for a screen, one of them took money on the door, and the other operated a projector.

Thus the business empire began!

As their first business had been relatively successful, the brothers decided to expand, so shortly afterwards, they leased their first cinema in Salford, which had been formerly a skating rink and ballroom,

Beloved Ghosts

but which had been converted into a cinema in 1911. After that, there was no stopping them, leasing cinema after cinema.

However, notwithstanding the success, Billy decided that the cinema business was not for him after all, as he did not like the responsibility.

He became a bus driver, but the two brothers always remained close.

He married a lady called Mary Anne, who came from Alderley Edge in Cheshire. Unfortunately, he strayed, and produced an illegitimate daughter.

Her name was Miss Jump.

Grandfather's other brother, Harry, fought through the First World War, survived, bemedaled, but unscathed, and went back to work as a clerk for the railways.

His sister, Winifred, married a butcher and went to live in Anglesey.

During this time, grandfather continued to acquire cinemas, solely on short term leases, as he did not have the necessary capital to invest in purchasing them.

He also became a local councillor in Salford, thus his political and business careers started at roughly the same time.

The early days of cinema must have been a delightful adventure, a thriving industry, with little or no regulation.

Grandfather had a cinema in Manchester, which employed a full orchestra to play accompanying music, and fill in during the intervals.

On one occasion, a circus film was being shown, and so a full circus parade, complete with elephants, strong men and jugglers, was organised to roam the streets of Manchester to publicise the film.

From 1924 onwards, for the next 25 years or thereabouts, he acquired nearly 100 cinemas in places as diverse as Bradford, Blackpool, Bristol, Cardiff, Derby, Lincoln, Huddersfield, Peterbrough, Westbury and Wimbledon.

The Vista cinema in Westbury had the most beautiful hand painted ceiling the style of a Roman Church. This cinema continued until the 1980's, although not in the ownership of my grandfather, until, in late 1988 the building was damaged by fire, and only the facade remained standing. This was subsequently demolished, leaving only memories.

Personal appearances by stars were quite common, although they were not of the glamorous Hollywood variety. I remember Frank Randle making an appearance at the Empire Cinema in Blackpool. Joan Greenwood and Jimmy Hanley attended a cinema ball in the Winter Gardens Ballroom, Blackpool, in 1949, as 'Guests of Honour'.

Just a couple of reminiscences about the cinema business. Do you remember that virtually every cinema used to have a uniformed doorman or commissionaire? The uniform was like something out of a light opera, lots of braid, epaulettes and medals. Do not forget as well, the usherettes with the all seeing torch...how they used to trip down the aisle at the interval selling ice cream. There were usually two main features, a B movie to support the main feature, sometimes a newsreel, and, always, the trailer for the next week, or even for the next three days, as programmes often changed twice a week. There were no cinema showings on Sundays, unless the Local Authority permitted it following a local poll, and certainly nothing could be shown before 7 pm.

The cinema business was one long success story until the advent of television, when almost overnight the whole business collapsed. Audiences dwindled, cinema leases were not renewed, and many were turned over to bingo.

Just to show that my grandfather's business judgement was not infallible. Apparently he was asked by one of the Bernstein brothers if he would like to come into a business venture with them, which they were just starting. The business venture was in fact, Granada Television. My grandfather declined on the basis that he did not think commercial television would last! I think that was just wishful thinking on his behalf!

Parallel with the cinema business, grandfather was pursuing a political career.

He recalled many boyhood discussions with his father on the politics of the time of his youth. They were the days of the rule of the privileged classes, and the injustice of this stayed with him, although he was a firm believer in private enterprise and fair competition. So it is perhaps not surprising that in 1921 we find him elected a Tory councillor in Salford, becoming, in 1923, the Leader of the Council. Ten years later, his adopted City of Salford showed him its appreciation by making him Mayor.

In 1935, he was elected Conservative MP for Salford West, and served 10 years, covering the hectic and historical days of the Abdication Crisis and the War. He served under three Prime Ministers, Baldwin, Chamberlain, and Churchill, meeting most of the leading figures of the day, both at home and abroad. He was a member of a various parliamentary delegations, which took him to Egypt, France, Belgium and Germany, where prior to Munich, he met Hitler, Göring and Goebbels, and others of that infamous gang. He stood feet from Hitler at the 1937 Nuremberg rally, having gone to Germany to see what could be learned from the construction of the German Autobahns.

He considered Lloyd George to be the greatest orator in Parliament, far surpassing Churchill and Aneurin Bevan.

On a personal note, he also thought that Edward VIII was a most unsuitable man as an individual and as a King, and he was delighted when Edward abdicated, allowing his brother, George, to take over. He subsequently attended George's coronation in 1938.

My grandfather was also present when one of the most important Parliamentary debates took place, culminating in two of the most memorable speeches ever made. The Norway debate, as it was called, took place between the 7th and 9th May, 1940, approximately three weeks before the evacuation from Dunkirk, from which my own father came home.

At this time, Neville Chamberlain was still Prime Minister, and, by and large a popular politician.

On the 9th April 1940, Germany had invaded neutral Norway. In response to the invasion, Britain sent limited land and naval forces to assist the Norwegians, but apart from a relatively minor naval success at Narvik, the rest of the campaign went very badly for Britain, with many casualties.

The debate in the House of Commons was really a simple motion to adjourn the House, but it developed into a scathing criticism of the conduct of the war, and of Mr Chamberlain, in particular. Eventually, it became clear that it was to become a vote of confidence in the Government.

Member after member criticised the conduct of the war cabinet until eventually a former cabinet minister, Leo Amery, delivered the fatal blow.

He made a long speech, reasoned and impassioned, which culminated in the following words: "I have quoted certain words of Oliver Cromwell. I will quote certain other words. I do it with great reluctance as I am speaking of those who are old friends and associates of mine, but they are words, which I think are applicable to the present situation. This is what Cromwell said to the Long Parliament when he thought that it was no longer fit to conduct the affairs of the nation: 'You have sat too long here for any good you have been doing. Depart I say, and let us have done with you. In the name of God, go'".

Lloyd George afterwards told Amery that, in fifty years, he had heard few speeches that matched his in sustained power, and none with so dramatic a climax.

From that moment on, Chamberlain's fate was sealed, and although he won what was in effect a vote of confidence by 281 votes to 200 (a majority of 81) the Governments notional majority was, in fact, 213. 41 members voted with the opposition, whilst an estimated 60 other Conservatives abstained. Rebels sang *Rule Britannia* and there were loud cries of "go!" as Chamberlain left the House.

My grandfather voted with Chamberlain, and for the Government.

Following that vote, Chamberlain attempted to form a National Coalition Government, but eventually Churchill emerged as the probable new Prime Minister, Clement Atlee having made it clear that he would not serve in a war time cabinet under Chamberlain, but would do so under Churchill.

On the 13th May, Churchill returned to the House and made his famous "I have nothing to offer but blood, toil, tears and sweat" speech.

The House voted on his appointment, which was endorsed without opposition.

Thus, history was made and somehow we, as a nation, were on the road to salvation, although it did not seem like it at the time.

There was an apocryphal tale that following Leo Amery's speech of betrayal, his family suffered bad luck thereafter. This was not altogether true, though Leo Amery's elder son, John, became an open Nazi sympathiser and was hanged for treason after the war.

Beloved Ghosts

During his time in Parliament, grandfather also sat on the committee which formed the basis of the future National Health Service, which the Labour government established in 1947. He was particularly proud to have sat on that committee, having seen such poverty and illness in his childhood.

In 1945, he stood for re-election, but was defeated in the Labour landslide of that year, and thus his political career came to an end.

While still a Member of Parliament, in 1942, he had purchased Illawalla, an extraordinary house, reputedly the biggest bungalow in Europe, complete with ten bedrooms, four bathrooms, billiard room, ballroom, a tower, a minaret, and a green copper dome, together with 15 acres of garden, paddocks and pastures. It was occupied by the Army at that time, but then became a convalescent home for pregnant refugees. Needless to say, it was in a need of substantial repair.

He purchased the property as a statement. A statement to himself that he had succeeded, and a statement of similar success to the world, although most of the world knew little or nothing of him, or his struggles, or his family background.

A few people knew him, of course – his employees, his constituents, his family, though even his own family had no idea what made grandfather so tenacious, and determined, indeed all the adjectives one could conceive to describe a man who had succeeded by chance, good luck, and sheer hard work.

Having a firm faith and fervent belief in God, grandfather would always acknowledge and thank God for his good luck. Later in life, he would pray aloud in the big house, especially on nights where the wind, howling off the Irish Sea, would rattle the dome, and sometimes tear the Union Jack from its mast on the very top of the building.

When you think about it, it was an astonishing statement of confidence by him, as in 1942 it was by no means certain which way the war would go.

The house itself was quite extraordinary. It was built in 1902, the foundation stone being laid by Vesta Tilley whose real name was Matilda Alice Powles, born in 1864 in Worcester. She first appeared on stage at the age of six, and was so well known that by the age of eleven, she supported her parents and the rest of her family.

She became a male impersonator, creating many characters, the most famous being Burlington Bertie.

In 1890, she married Walter De Frece, a prominent theatrical manager and owner of several theatres.

He was also a director on the Alhambra Palace board in Blackpool. The Alhambra eventually became the famous Palace, which was acquired by the Blackpool Tower Company in 1903, remodelled by famous theatre architect Frank Matcham and reopened as The Palace in 1904. It was eventually demolished in 1961, replaced with a Lewis's department store.

So in 1902, at the time of the laying of the foundation stone, Walter De Frece was on the board of the Alhambra Palace and married to Vesta Tilley.

He was also a friend of Clement Vincent Howarth (born 1856), the man who conceived the idea of Illawalla, and who eventually built it. Apparently, he designed the property himself after an indulgent evening, and a night of wild dreams.

Clement Howarth was also a director on the Blackpool Alhambra Palace board, and that is how he came to ask Walter De Frece to suggest to his wife, Vesta Tilley, that she lay the foundation stone.

It is amazing how one can go off at a tangent when researching, and I ended up finding out that Walter De Frece, who was eventually knighted, was elected a Conservative MP for Ashton-Under-Lyne at a by-election in 1920, and was re-elected in the General Elections of 1922 and 1923.

In the General Election of 1924, he moved his loyalty to Blackpool, and became its MP with a large majority.

His loyalty was all that he moved, as he decided to live in Monte Carlo. He only visited the United Kingdom twice a year, once for the Budget and once for Royal Ascot.

He managed to convince his Blackpool electorate that he was representing their interests by signing a stack of House of Commons notepaper each time he came back to England, making it appear to the voters that they had each received a personal response.

He never actually went to Blackpool, and was reputed to have said that he could not even find it on a map.

On those facts alone, today's press would have a field day.

Beloved Ghosts

In 1920, the ownership of Illawalla transferred from Mr Howarth to a Mr Ernest Broadbelt, a wholesale vegetable and fruit merchant from Manchester, who owned it until it was requisitioned by the Army, from whom grandfather eventually purchased it, midway through the war.

Ernest Broadbelt was an interesting man. He was an agent for Manchester's Smithfield market in 1897, from where he began a successful and profitable flower and fruit business.

His company had a warehouse larger than any of its competitors. It became the biggest supplier of cut flowers in the United Kingdom, and was also the sole importer into England of Fyffe's bananas.

So, at the end of the war in 1945, we have a battered country, shortages of everything, rationing, a dilapidated house in urgent need of repair, with a vigorous owner sixty years young, ready and willing and financially able to take on the burden of refurbishing an extraordinary property.

The period of refurbishment took over a year, labour and materials being in such short supply at that time, grandfather finally taking possession in 1946. It was his home for over 40 years, and for about 20 of those years, it was my home as well.

In 1957, as a result of his service on the Parliamentary National Health Committee, and a lifetime of public service he was knighted and became Sir Frederick Emery.

So the young man who once collected the tickets at Gathurst Station was now a knight of the realm, honoured by his Queen and honoured by his adopted city of Salford.

My grandfather was an amazing man and he lived a long and fulfilled life, although like everyone else, he suffered tragedies, particularly, in the loss of three sons. His infant son, Freddie, was only eighteen months old, when he died of influenza. He subsequently lost his son Ronnie, in the fall of Singapore, and his son Gordon, to prostate cancer, many years after the war.

In the early sixties, his granddaughter Valerie, my sister, was killed in a tragic coach accident. In another motor accident, his grandson Bobby was killed outside Arnold School in Blackpool. Apparently Bobby had run out into the road without looking, and the poor driver had no chance to stop.

As a true businessman, he never really retired and continued with his interests in business and politics, until his death in 1982 at the age of 96.

In 1977, my grandfather who by then was 91 decided that he had enough of the big house, the cost of upkeep was too much, and he was too old to enjoy the gardens and grounds, although occasionally he would wander down and watch Thornton Cleveleys play cricket.

After selling Illawalla my grandfather went to live with my parents in Cleveleys, where he lived another 5 years in great comfort and at peace.

One day he decided that he did not want to get out of bed and was feeling tired. He remained there for several weeks and eventually slipped away. This is how my mother saw his last days:

Thank you very much for your lovely letter of sympathy and also for your kind donation to the Blackpool Hospice in memory of my dear father.
It is very difficult to explain to other people just what my father meant to me. From being a little girl, and later as an adult, I always looked up to him as someone so very special. He was so wise and his influence will stay with me as long as I live.
I will try in every way possible to emulate his example.
He was ill in bed for 16 weeks with a rapid and irregular heart action. The doctor hoped he'd be able to control it with drugs, but sadly they had no effect on him and as the weeks passed he knew, and I knew, that his days were numbered. Still, he fought on doing everything he was told, but I could see him visibly ageing day by day.
The last week he was disturbed and uncomfortable and for the first time he acknowledged he was tired and weary, and ready to meet his Maker.

Beloved Ghosts

He was nearly 97 and had lived his life to the full. But now he was blind and deaf and unable to walk more than a few steps.
There was really nothing for him to look forward to except pain and suffering.
I was sitting by his bedside holding his hand as he drew his last breath and passed peacefully over to the other side.
Now he is at peace with mother, my three brothers, Valerie and little Bobby, and a host of other relatives and friends.
Much as I loved him I couldn't be so cruel as to wish him back.
I shall just cherish his memory and thank God I was lucky enough to be born his daughter.
Mr Taylor and I are now on our own for the first time in 45 years and trying to adjust to what is, for us, a strange new life.
We both thank God that we, are blessed with good children and beautiful grandchildren.
With many thanks for your thoughtfulness,
Margaret Taylor

When my mother heard him stop breathing, she kissed him, turned off the electric clock to show what time he had died and left him at peace.

No man could have had a more loving daughter, though that love greatly affected my parents' marriage.

Mother was always caught between father's resentment and jealousy, and her preferred duty and love for her father.

Grandfather always admitted that he was a lucky man in the way he lived. He was also lucky in the way he died, no disease, little pain, just a slight disturbance at the end. He deserved a calm death.

After his death, my mother received over 200 letters and cards of sympathy.

CHAPTER 6. ILLAWALLA, THE HOUSE

The property was built around a central hall measuring 70 ft by 40 ft. As one entered through the massive front doors, the hall was displayed in front of you in all its glory. It was reached down a short flight of steps and was surrounded on three sides by a gallery, divided into bays by mahogany pillars, and if necessary, could be cut off from the rest of the house by damask curtaining.

The wall space was richly embossed by hundreds of rose medallions, with a moulding covered in pure leaf gold.

All the surrounding walls were beautifully decorated with frescoes and murals, and the wooden pillars were elaborately carved.

In the centre of the hall there stood a table, which originally came from the Tsar's Palace in St. Petersburg.

On one of the walls there was a painting of a Russian hunting scheme by the Polish artist Wychert.

A series of couches and divans filled the floor space, one in delicate gleaming satin originally owned by a Princess of Pless.

Standing on ebony and bronze cabinets filled with rare china were two large vases, hand painted by Deprcz, bearing the initial "N" which could be rotated on their base to reveal Napoleon's battles in separately painted scenes.

There were graceful writing desks of the early French period, including a Louis XVI bureau with a miniature of Marie Antoinette on one of its drawers. There was also a writing table with superbly painted panels of Sevres porcelain inset in bronze.

Off the central hall, there were various rooms, including a library, a dining room, lounge, and three bedrooms.

The dining room contained some wonderful paintings- a portrait of Catherine of Braganza by Sir Peter Lely; a portrait of Sidney Earl of Godolphin by Kneller; a study of Lady Hamilton by Romney; and Holbein's forceful head of a Duke of Sutherland contrasting with the Boy with Apples by Millais. This study was reputed to be the counterpart of Millais' famous study entitled Bubbles.

The dining room also contained a cleverly disguised motto above the fireplace recess, which displayed a parrot above the intertwined letters "S" and "T". The message was simply: 'on ST, pol (the parrot) I see'. Honesty is the best policy.

Adjacent to the dining room was the lounge, or drawing room, with its original brocade-like wallpaper, which grandfather was told could never be matched.

In the lounge, there was a portrait of Louis Pisani, a pupil of Carlo Dolci of Florence, and a copy of Dolci's famous "Poetry", which is said by many critics to equal, if not outshine the original.

Another treasure was a unique porcelain sideboard by Turner of Tunstall, painted with scenes illustrating Charles Kingsley's famous poem "The Three Fishers". Both words and music in 18 carat gold were intertwined with hand painted scenes in which the three fishermen are symbolised by three flowers.

Against the original brocade light wallpaper stood two tall cyclamen coloured Sevres vases. In harmony with the opulent richness of the room, heavily ornamented cabinets of ebony red lacquer and bronze (from the Glasgow Exhibition of 1886) contrasted vibrantly with the blue velvet of chairs from the Coronation of King George VI and Queen Elizabeth.

Next to the lounge, was the library where there was a striking portrait of Sir Winston Churchill. Among the many books, there were bound volumes of the Strand magazine, which contained the original Sherlock Holmes stories.

At the back of the house, there was a billiard room, framed with beautiful stained glass windows with sporting themes. Built originally for Illawalla, the full sized billiard table was, at one point, sold to a hotel in Matlock, but was brought back to the house. The room also contained pictures of sporting interests and a collection of photographs of racehorses formerly owned by my grandfather.

A regular visitor to the house (and the billiard room) was Sir Gordon Richards, the former champion jockey, who rode many of the 17 racehorses grandfather had in training at Newmarket.

Another visitor was Tom Reece, the six times runner up in the World Billiards Championship. According to Google, he was the holder of the world record billiards' break of 499,135, which took him five weeks using an anchor or cradle cannon nurse system.

One of grandfather's horses, Ugongo, created something of a sensation when going down to the start of the 1949 Epsom Derby. He became trapped in a gate which had been left on the ground, and had to be destroyed. Shard Bridge was another famous horse under my grandfather's ownership.

Outside, there were extensive gardens requiring the services of anything between three and ten gardeners.

There was a grassed tennis court, and a fully graded bowling green – with an appropriate crown.

There was also a rock garden, together with hot houses, cold greenhouses, stabling for three horses, and a summer house on each lawn.

A large meadow behind the rock garden led down to the River Wyre, with wonderful views across the estuary.

In the 1950's grandfather had been persuaded by Tom Crelling, his physiotherapist, to lease the meadow to Thornton Cleveley's Cricket Club for a period of 60 years at an annual peppercorn rent of £5.

The Cricket Club was established as soon as possible thereafter, and continues to play at the Illawalla ground to this day.

Eventually in 1997, long after grandfather had sold Illawalla, the freehold was purchased by the cricket club, from the then owner of Illawalla, David McGrath.

Thanks to the original generosity of my grandfather, the future of the local cricket club was secured.

CHAPTER 7. ILLAWALLA, THE CONTINUING STORY

Late in 1977, my grandfather was approached by a local businessman Tim Kilpatrick who owned the Buccaneer Inn, formerly Thornton Lodge, just down the road from Illawalla.

About this time, Ken Russell the film director, through his locations manager, Richard Green (another Richard Green, not the actor who played Robin Hood) was out and about looking for suitable locations for the film 'Valentino'. He had heard about Illawalla but did not know exactly where it was. He came into the Buccaneer and asked for directions. As a result of that chance meeting, Tim became interested in Illawalla and following negotiations he eventually purchased it in March 1978.

Throughout his dealings with my grandfather, who was then 91, Tim was always courteous and considerate, and I thank him for that.

A brief diversion about the film "Valentino". It was of course, very loosely based, in part, on the life of Rudolf Valentino. It starred Rudolf Nureyev, Leslie Caron, Michelle Phillips and Felicity Kendall.

It was a critical and commercial failure, and Ken Russell later described his decision to make the film as the biggest mistake of his career.

It was so bad that instead of starring Leslie Caron and Michelle Phillips, it should have just starred Leslie Phillips!

Several scenes were shot in Illawalla, including a scene in the centre hall, which doubled as a hotel lobby.

Many local people were hired as extras, and Tim and Hazel were able to supply much of the catering from the Buccaneer.

When the filming was finished, Tim entered into negotiations with my grandfather, and eventually they reached an agreement on a sale.

After he had completed the purchase, Tim had the idea of turning Illawalla into a Country Club, but, of course, he needed a Licence, so he found fifty likeminded gentlemen and obtained the necessary permission which included a Licence for music, singing and dancing. It costs £25.00 to be a life member and eventually there were 1000 members. The Country Club was elegant and provided dinner dances. It opened to a blaze of publicity on August 14th 1978, and was instantly popular. In addition to the facilities within the club, there was also a Tennis Court, a croquet lawn and beautiful gardens to walk in.

Initially it was a great success, but unfortunately the boom did not last, and a change of direction was necessary.

John Barnett, Tim's advisor and friend, later to be appointed a Lord Lieutenant of Lancashire, suggested that Tim emulate the famous Studio 54 in New York, and open one night per week as a very different type of club. He proposed membership at £5.00 per year, and eventually opened in that format at Easter 1979. Very shortly, he had 3000 members and it was an amazing success.

From one night a week, it then expanded to Thursdays, Fridays and Saturdays. It was the "in place" to go. He organised birthday nights, charity tombola nights, weddings, beauty contests. The club was visited by all the stars performing in Blackpool, and was packed every night.

At the height of the club's popularity, it had its own football teams, a roller skating rink, and an exhibition centre.

Also, as a result of this success, Tim was able to open other hostelries in the area, including The Musketeer at Cleveleys and The Bounty in St Annes.

However, Tim and his family were working themselves to death running the place, and reinvesting all the profits in continuous refurbishment and improvements.

Boom times are usually followed by a recession, and this was the case with Illawalla and its night life. Tim eventually sold out to Boddingtons Brewery in 1985. Boddingtons tried to operate the club, but had no club experience being solely pub operators, and so in 1987 the property was put on the market and notwithstanding the efforts to save Illawalla as a building of historical interest, it was eventually sold for housing development in 1992.

As an aside, the singer Glyn Bailey recorded "Songs from the Old Illawalla".

I wrote to Glyn and asked him for his personal experiences of Illawalla. He very kindly replied, and told me that he had been looking for a concept for his second album, the artwork for which consisted of old

Beloved Ghosts

Music Hall programmes from the 1920/1930's. At that time, his daughter was going out with a young man who lived in one of the new houses built when Illawalla was demolished. The name struck him as being unusual, and a great name for a fantasy music hall, with the addition of "Old", so songs from the Old Illawalla came into being.

Unfortunately none of the songs on the album were actually about Illawalla!!

Later on, Glyn wrote a further song called "The Old Illawalla" which featured on his third album. The song was a fantasy about finding a buried chest in the ruins of Illawalla, and the consequences for the finder.

A photographer named Rebecca Velvet produced a photograph of a wrecked sailing boat. She called it 'Haunting the Illawalla'. The location of the wreck seemed to be Skippool Creek, which flowed from the River Wyre, immediately adjacent to the ground occupied by Thornton Clevely's cricket club. I think it is a stunning photograph, whatever the location, and can be seen on the Internet.

CHAPTER 8. LIVING AT ILLAWALLA

I lived at Illawalla with my parents and sisters for over twenty years, although for much of that time I was at boarding school.

My sisters were also at boarding school, and as the house was so big, we were like ships that passed in the night, only getting together occasionally at mealtimes, or on festive occasions.

I thought it was normal to live in a house of that size as I had never really known anything else. My memories of the war-time house in Cleveleys were very hazy, so I assumed that everybody lived in the same way. This thought was reinforced by the neighbours' surrounding houses, which were fairly substantial, standing within large grounds.

I went to boarding school aged eight, and therefore, never saw how other people lived. It was only when I left school that I realised what a privileged existence I had enjoyed.

Within Illawalla, all the rooms were enormous. We were summoned for meals by a gong sounded by grandfather's butler (who had been my father's batman in the war). We all trooped to the dining room where the overworked butler waited on us.

At 4 o'clock every day, afternoon tea was served by, yes, the butler, who wheeled in a trolley with all the usual things that all people, everywhere, every day, have for afternoon tea- cakes, scones, toast, jam, tea or coffee, etc!

There were other employees, maids, cooks, etc, and of course, several gardeners.

You can imagine the contrast of going from that home environment to a monastic boarding school where one's personal space was limited to sharing a room with two or three other people and a very hard single bed.

My encounters with real life and real people only began when I joined the local rugby and tennis clubs, and I found out that what I thought was normal was, in fact, not normal at all.

I did my best to share my good fortune with as many people as possible, but I could not have had a more bizarre childhood, either at boarding school or living in a huge mansion, with servants and with a father who resented every moment of living there, and who was determined to eliminate any softness in my nature.

I have many memories of living at Illawalla. For example, take an average Christmas Day... average!?

The centre hall would be decorated in the usual way for the festive season. In the middle of the hall was the most enormous Christmas tree, reaching to the glass ceiling, covered in decorations, of course, with the traditional fairy at the top, and stacks of presents underneath. All the family aunts, uncles, cousins and their children were involved.

The day started at 10 am with the sight of the local brass band walking up the long front drive to eventually end up in the centre hall, where they played Christmas carols.

No chance of a lie in then!

Next, all the children were ordered to stand in the window of one of the main rooms overlooking the lawns and gardens.

Then, from behind the trees came Father Christmas, walking across the lawn dragging a huge sledge piled high with presents.

As children, you can imagine our excitement when it came to the opening of the presents.

I was not to be given a present until Father Christmas had been assured by my mother that I had been a good boy throughout the year.

Then, into the dining room for lunch, cooked and served by, yes, you guessed it, the butler.

Adults sat at one table, children sat at another and it was absolute bliss when I was told that I, as the eldest, could sit at the adults' table.

Finally, full of lunch and fuelled by alcohol (the adults, not the children), we all retired to the main hall for party games and to listen to the King's Speech.

How privileged! How perfect.

Christmas at home made such an impression on me that for years I believed in Father Christmas.

I remember defending his existence at school, when I was 10. One boy said that he must have been one of my uncles, dressed up. I spent the rest of the day ticking off the names of my uncles to make sure they were all present!

CHAPTER 9. THE START TO MY LEGAL CAREER

No boring stories about cases, conveyances, damages or writs, I promise you!

I left school on December 12th 1957, and on December the 13th 1957, I started work as an Articled Clerk to the Town Clerk of Blackpool, Mr. Ernest Lee.

I remember my articled clerkship with great affection, not least because of the kindness shown to me by James Swaffield, a solicitor in his thirties who was the deputy Town Clerk. We always had a laugh, and he followed my rugby career with interest. James Swaffield was destined to become a man of great distinction. After a career in local government, he became Secretary of the Association of Municipal Corporations and from 1973, Director General of the Greater London Council.

He was also clerk to the Inner London Education Authority, and became involved in the dispute between Ken Livingstone and Margaret Thatcher. He finally retired from local government in 1984 with a "mixture of relief and regret".

He then became a successful chairman of the British Rail Property Board.

He had been appointed a CBE in 1971, and was knighted in 1976.

He was a lovely man to work with. Then, we were just 'Jim and David'.

Back to the story. Father had to pay a £500 premium to the Blackpool Corporation for the privilege of my being taught the law. My salary was precisely zero.

I was placed in an office with a venerable (or so it seemed to me) gentleman of great experience, a Mr. Horace Cook.

He was to be my mentor for what was intended to be a five-year clerkship. He was an expert in all conveyancing matters.

He was a really nice man, though his supervisory powers were nil. He could not think of anything to give me that he could not do himself in half the time.

He gave me a warning, "David, whatever you do, never make a decision!".

When I enquired why, he said that the decision might rebound on the Mayor Aldermen and Burgesses of the Borough of Blackpool, with a consequential effect on our respective careers.

He did however find one job for me.

I was to supervise the allocation of grave spaces in Blackpool's Municipal Cemetery.

Anyone who came into the Town Clerk's office to buy a grave space was directed to me. I seem to remember that the fee was ten shillings, and on payment of that sum, I allocated a grave space in perpetuity and gave an appropriate receipt.

Many of the people I saw were upset, and desperately anxious to ensure that they would be buried next to or near to their loved ones. I did my best to accommodate them.

That was my first experience of dealing with the public.

Another advantage of being articled to the Town Clerk was the location of the Town Hall office, just down the road from the Blackpool Tower ballroom. Some afternoons of unsupervised work became afternoons of delight, as I sneaked off down the road to attend the afternoon tea dances. I thought I was the bee's knees, dressed in my uncle's demob suit, which was at that time at least 12 years old, and a sort of pinkish shade.

As well as the afternoon dance sessions, the Town Hall legal staff was full of beautiful young ladies. There was I, from the monastic existence of a boys' only boarding school, surrounded by dozens of members of the very fair sex.

I remember Betty, Sylvia, Audrey and Frieda, all with affection, assisting, as they did, with my transition into manhood.

One day a week, I was supposed to attend Law lectures at the local Technical College.

The College had inept, but kind, lecturers who were no match for 20 or so relatively rumbustious youths.

Our knowledge of Law was scarcely enhanced, but we benefitted the College's rugby team, and its several drinking societies.

However, whilst being articled to the Town Clerk was akin to attending a holiday camp, I realised that I

Beloved Ghosts

was learning nothing, although my dancing and drinking were nearly perfect.

I resigned, and arranged with the Law Society for the balance of my articles to be transferred to a legal firm run by a friend in Lytham St Annes.

Permit me here to be a little nostalgic.

I was in my teens, early twenties. I was growing up and spending my days and some nights in what, to me, was the most exciting place on earth, Blackpool.

I hear you scoff and mock, but Blackpool in the late 50's and early 60's was magic time.

I could easily go on the Internet and discover which shows, stars, films and variety bills were in town during that time, but that would be cheating.

These are *my* personal memories.

Of course, other people will have other memories, but maybe some of my reminiscences will strike a chord and happiness may come flooding back.

I remember David Whitfield singing Cara Mia at the Opera House, and bowing to his lady who was sitting in the royal box; Josef Locke singing at the Queens Theatre, parading up and down the aisles, between the seats, ladies garments being thrown at him; Nat Jackley rubbernecking it; Glenn Melvyn, Arthur Askey and Danny Ross at the Grand Theatre – silly, stupid, wonderful farces; the Bernard Brothers at the Opera House; Jimmy Jewel and Ben Warriss in a show called Coconut Grove at the Hippodrome, where I had the pleasure of seeing my first topless (but stationary) lady; I remember a young Shirley Bassey at the Opera House; Tessie O'Shea; Winifred Atwell; Dave Morris on South Pier; Arthur Haynes; the beautiful Yana; Eddie Calvert and Oh Mein Papa; Ken Dodd; Joan Regan; Lita Roza.

Not only were there the theatres and the stars, there were also about half a dozen cinemas, some of them family owned, all within walking distance.

I remember sneaking off to the Palace Cinema to see the Jolson Story… the booming voice, no introduction, straight into Jolson singing. I was hooked.

So these were just my memories. Is sentimentality a weakness? Not to me, I am continually transported back to those happy times filled with music and laughter.

As Scott Fitzgerald said in his famous ending to the Great Gatsby, "So we beat on, boats against the current, borne back ceaselessly into the past".

CHAPTER 10. FATHER

Father's scrapbook was like his life.

A jumble of memories with no particular order or organisation.

He puts a letter from 1920 in the same section as his Magistrates Service in 1953. A report of my accident in Guildford, he puts with his win in a local council election.

His Matriculation certificate from 1930, is mixed in with a report of a rugby game in which I was playing.

Many pictures of his old friends are mixed in with theatre programmes. Cruise passenger lists are interleaved with Rotary Club reports.

Running through the whole book is a feeling of gloom.

He put pictures of all the Magistrates who were appointed with him or who sat with him, and one by one he would put a cross by them as they died.

Contrary to my perception, he appeared to have taken an interest in my rugby career as there were several cuttings about me. I am surprised he did not put a cross against those articles.

He had a huge inferiority complex, mainly brought on by the fact that my mother's father was very rich, and very successful. He employed my father, as well as providing a house for him and my mother.

Whatever the circumstances of his family and employment, they certainly contributed to the later life catastrophe that occurred.

Father was born in 1914, in Thames Ditton. His father was a mechanical engineer and printing machinery salesman, but mother Rose was the controller, a martinet, and the family matriarch. She ordered the lives of my father and his sister, Mary. Yes, the same Mary who wanted to fight the Boche, and whose holidays were "dished" by Hitler.

My memories of my paternal grandmother are mixed. She tried to teach me the piano, but did it in such a way that I hated it, and I gave it up as soon as I could. However, she or father (himself a superb pianist) somehow imbued in me love of music, and I returned to my piano in my late teenage years and never really stopped thereafter.

Rose, or "Grandma Tay" as she was known, lived with Mary and Mary's husband Ian, in a smallish house in Blackpool. Ian was a kindly, moustachioed man, a radio ham, with a room full of knobs and dials, switches and aerials, sticking out at all angles.

The whole family (Mary, Ian, and daughter Elizabeth) eventually moved to Huddersfield. Ian worked as a television engineer, and he was the man who switched on the Yorkshire TV Holme Moss transmitter. Years later, as a sort of recognition, he was asked to perform the final switch off, when the transmitter was closed down.

We visited Grandma Tay every Saturday and, to compensate for my boredom, she always bought two comics for me, "The Wizard" and "The Hotspur"... oh, Limp Along Leslie and the Magnificent Wilson of my early teenage years!

I saw little of Grandma Tay after they moved to Huddersfield. The wheel, eventually, went full circle, as one of my first jobs as a solicitor was to wind up her Estate. There was not much, and all went to Father and Mary. Her will ended with the words "... and my ashes scattered to the four winds".

One of father's passions was music, having being taught to play the piano by his mother. There are pianists who just play, and pianists who are sublime entertainers. Father was one of the latter breed.

He could listen to a radio, and immediately pick out the key of the tune that was being played, and then join in on the piano.

In 1930, when he was aged 16, he formed his own group called "Bob Taylor's Rhythm Boys", and the group used to play at various local dances.

I have various dance programmes from what I would call "the dance band years" and it is interesting to see the engagement cards where one could reserve a partner for a foxtrot or a veleta. I am not certain when he ceased playing for money, but he played the piano every day throughout his life, and as my parents early marriage days coincided with the time where more or less every household had a piano, father was always very popular everywhere he went.

Beloved Ghosts

Father also tried to play rugby, joining Sedgeley Park, but I can see no cuttings relating to his playing days except the following:
'In the match at Fallowfield, in which Manchester University Faculty of Technology beat Sedgeley Park by 13 points to nothing. R.E. Taylor, a Sedgeley Park back, had his collar bone broken".

Poor father, the paper could not even get his initials right, as he was Robert Charles, so his initials would be R.C., and he was only mentioned because he was injured.

We are still in the early 1930's, when father was in his late teens. My mother, in fact, lived just around the corner in Salford. Margaret Winifred Pauline Emery was the daughter of the local Mayor, who in 1935 was elected to be the Conservative Member of Parliament for Salford West.

I am not certain how they met (although one story has it, that they met at school when mother was 6 years old), but meet they did, and all the later tragedies of their lives stemmed from that moment.

After four to five years of courtship, no doubt heavily supervised, it was decided that father would be a suitable match for mother. Did he have any say in the matter? Probably not.

It had to be a big wedding. A major social event in Salford in 1938. A telegram from Mrs. Neville Chamberlain, the Prime Minister's wife. Coverage on Pathé news. Three hundred and fifty guests. An enormous crowd at the church.

They went on honeymoon to Brittany. They then set up home in Reading, where father worked as a printer, and where I was eventually born.

He joined the Territorial Army on the 27th April 1939, and enlisted in the Berkshire Regiment of the Royal Engineers. Clearly he volunteered, but there is no one to ask why he volunteered. Was it on the advice of my grandfather who was a Member of Parliament, and who would clearly have an inkling that war might not be long off?

He was called up as soon as war was declared on 3rd September 1939.

On 31st October 1939, he was appointed an Acting Lance Corporal, and on the 5th January 1940 he embarked to Europe with the British Expeditionary Force. He landed in France on the 6th January 1940.

He attended a Mechanical Engineers course in February 1940, presumably in France, and then came back to England to attend a Motor Transport Course at Chatham.

Now a full Lance Corporal, he was sent back to France via Dover on the 7th April 1940.

He was part of the retreat to Dunkirk from which he eventually returned around the 29th May 1940. He says that he came off the beaches, and somehow boarded a destroyer, though he could not remember the name of the ship, nor much about the actual evacuation. Of course, I should have pressed him for more details, but I was a young lad and unaware of the importance of Dunkirk in our history.

As I grew older, I reached a stage where father and I spoke very little, so my opportunity to learn more was lost.

On arrival in England he sent a telegram to my mother. It was the master of British understatement. All it said was **"Safe in England – Bob".**

He would never talk about his Dunkirk experience. A true Brit, with a stiff upper lip. Very much "Don't mention the war."

I was too scared of him to ask about his experiences. How I regret that now.

Appointed a Corporal on the 6th October 1940, he was then very quickly promoted to Acting Lance Sergeant with a final promotion to Sergeant on the 7th July 1941.

He was posted to Officer Cadet Training Unit on the 20th November 1941 and was appointed a Second Lieutenant on the 23rd May 1942. At the time of his appointment he was posted to the Royal Armoured Corps, the 79th Armoured Division, known as Hogan's Funnies.

He seems to have been a glutton for work and during the period 1942 to 1944 he attended courses on Compass Reading, Gunnery, Tanks, Mines, Tank Crew Commanders, Tactical School and Explosives. He was either anxious to learn, or nobody knew what to do with him.

Although his regiment saw action on D Day, I do not think that father was involved on the actual day itself, as reticent as he was, he would surely have mentioned it. He did however tell me of being chased across a field in France by a German fighter plane, whose pilot was attempting to kill him. He says he remembers the noise of the plane, and the sound of the bullets hitting the earth until he dived into a ditch. Whether that was when he was originally in France in 1940, or after D-Day, I do not know.

Beloved Ghosts

His next recorded posting was to the Divisional Headquarters of the British Liberation Army on 3rd March 1945.

Ahead of him, just over a month away, was the experience which was to affect his whole life.

His scrapbook is full of comments and praise as to his abilities on the various courses he attended.

Without doubt, he clearly needed the Army, and the Army, clearly, needed him.

I suspect that throughout this time he was happy, exhausting his quota of happiness, past and future, in what was after all a necessary war.

In April 1945, he was one of the earliest troops into Belsen.

He wrote to my grandfather who was a Member of Parliament at the time, and the letter is produced here:

"22.4.1945

Many of you will already have read in the newspapers everything I have to tell you here of the horrors of Belsen Concentration Camp, but because there are cynics among us and also because some of you may not have seen the newspapers, I am going to tell you what I myself have seen at Belsen. This account is not written with any idea of incitement to hatred but simply that each one of you shall have cold, objective realisation of the problem which confronts you.

It is perhaps symbolic that on the road some two miles from the camp, one of our party picked up a whip; a wooden handle with six leather thongs. Signposts were unnecessary. Our nostrils gave us the first intimation of our nearness. Those of you who were at Caen or Le Havre, or any other city which has suffered a shattering bombardment would have recognised the stench.

The first sight I saw while we were still outside the barbed wire was a completely nude woman in the open, who paid not the slightest attention to us, or the other males around. Rage and filth indescribable, bodies alive and dead, lay everywhere. I entered the camp. A soldier asked me if I could find a doctor as there was a woman imploring him to bring a doctor to her daughter who was dying. When the woman knew I spoke a little German she begged me to come with her, and find a doctor. I looked into the hut where her daughter was lying and no doctor on earth could have done anything for her. The mother herself had every sign of an early death written on her face.

While I was talking to this woman, another woman came out of a nearby hut and stooping astride a corpse to perform her natural functions on the corpse, entirely oblivious of the fact that we were only some ten yards away from her. Behind us was a canvas erection stacked high with female corpses.

Not far away I saw two children whose ages I guessed as seven to ten years. Their wrists and ankles were fleshless, their stomachs like balloons. One of these children was playing with a corpse as my son plays with an engine.

I saw a woman endeavouring to wash herself in a water trough. She was one of a line of a dozen, mostly males. Nobody paid the slightest attention to her nudity. I spoke to another woman who was endeavouring to clean herself with a cup full of water. I asked other officers what was their estimate of her age. The lowest guess was thirty-five. She had been taken there two years ago with her parents for listening to the BBC news. Her parents had been shot on the day of arrival and she had been there ever since. She was a German from Berlin. Her age was 17.

In the men's compound, a man lay on a plank and as we approached cried out for water, yet there was water not more than ten yards from him. He was too weak to get to it. There was no sanitation of any sort. People performed their natural functions anywhere. A man, clad in pyjamas, stepped out of a hut, and made an effort to pull down his pyjama trousers. He failed, and rolled over on the ground, to the best of my belief, dead. A Pole, who spoke English, said to me "a week ago this was Hell. Now it is Paradise. Like Johnny Walker, I still go strong. God save the King!" and with pathetic dignity, he strove to bring himself to attention and salute.

There are even allegations that prisoners ate the flesh of corpses. From the prisoners to whom I spoke, I got no confirmation of this, but I saw corpses one of whom had a slit stomach the other of whom had flesh missing from the thigh.

I saw only a small part of the whole camp, because my stomach revolted and I had to go.

Beloved Ghosts

THIS HAPPENED IN BELSEN IN GERMANY. YET BUT FOR THE GRACE OF GOD YOU MIGHT SUBSTITUTE BIRMINGHAM FOR BELSEN. THIS IS THE WORLDS THIRD CHANCE. WILL YOU TAKE IT?
Estimated 43,000 people here – Ron Evans reckons nearer 60,000 would be the figure. Apparently it is difficult to distinguish between the alive and the dead."

Who is to say what effect this had on him? Disturbingly, he brought a souvenir home from Belsen – the short, multi-strand whip, mentioned in the letter, and which had been clearly used. Maybe it is just today's sensitivities, unhardened by war, to assume such an item would not be appropriate as a souvenir. He kept it in his desk for years. Why?

So there we have a badly damaged man - having served throughout the war, having been in charge of men, and having seen the most horrendous sights - returning to normality, which meant being employed by my grandfather and living in a house which he did not own, and in the operation of which he had no say.

He was allocated a part of the garden for his own use. This was done with the best of intentions by my grandfather, but how demeaning for my father to be told, in effect, "These are your boundaries, stick to them."

It may be interesting to note that in the years 1942 to 1945 he only had a total of 90 days leave. I do not know whether that was a standard leave allocation or whether he just chose not to come home when he could. His experience in Belsen, and his general war experiences, would only have their effect in later years.

As has been mentioned, father had always been a keen pianist and performer and after peace was declared in May 1945, he remained in Europe as part of the Liberation Army until his eventual discharge. He visited Berlin and Hamburg, and saw all the devastation and human suffering.

Between May 1945 and November 1945 his main function appears to have been to organise entertainment for the troops who remained in occupation in Europe.

It is not known whether he volunteered to stay in Europe, or whether he was ordered to do so. My guess is that he volunteered.

He was a leading light in the Blackberries Concert party, and the Bags of Bull Roadshow which were the 79th Armoured Division's concert parties. They were described by Major General Sir Percy Hobart as the best concert parties he had ever seen. They toured the occupied war zones to alleviate the troop's boredom.

Father led the band, and a final tribute to him was when it featured in a broadcast on the Forces Network.

He was demobbed on the 20th November 1945 after a total war service of 6 years and 8 months, although after being demobbed, he remained on the reserve list until February 1946. At that time, he received a letter, which must have been sent to all discharged service personnel, thanking him for "the valuable services which he rendered in the time of grave national emergency".

He had left the war zone physically fit and well, an upright military man. He was also bad tempered, moody, and had great difficulty in showing any affection, except for and to his daughters. He did not speak of his war experiences, and I was not clever or brave enough to ask him. I was happy if I could avoid having to speak to him. How sad!

We now know that he would be suffering from Post Traumatic Stress Disorder, but of course in those days one just put up with it, with a stiff upper lip and the British attitude of "don't make a fuss".

CHAPTER 11. MY SISTER VALERIE – 1964

Let's pretend that my sisters' life is a play, a tragic farce.

She entered life stage left, and exited it some twenty years later, thrown down a mountainside.

My sister Valerie, she with the crinkly hair and the badly damaged face as mentioned in my visit to Guildford, was a wartime baby, born in 1943. She had the advantage of being a girl, consequently loved by my father. He could give her his love unconditionally, without feeling obliged to discipline her, or expect anything of her.

By contrast, his love for me was impossible effort, inherited no doubt from his mother and weak father. I assume that his father was weak, although I can never recall meeting him. I just assumed that he was weak because his wife, Grandma Tay, was so strong.

Picture her, Grandmother Tay, look at the strength in her face, the strain of growing up in the early years of the century, and then raising a family in the Depression.

What did father's father earn as a representative selling printing machinery? Was he happy? Did he have time to be happy? He only lived a few years, before dying of emphysema.

So here I am, wandering through the family archives, sitting in the sun wondering about my children. Of course, they think this age thing will never happen to them, and that they will sail through life.

So "where has it gone?", as it was only yesterday that I was 21, it was only yesterday that I became a father, it was only yesterday that I... oh, everything.

So reflections are paramount, yesterdays are remembered or forgotten. Time moves on. Tomorrow will be yesterday in the blink of an eye.

Back to Valerie. As I have said, a wartime baby, born in 1943, obviously a product of my father creeping around the house in the dead of night to sneak to my mother's bedroom.

She was christened Valerie Florence Taylor on November 20th 1943 at All Hallows Church, Bispham, near Blackpool.

She started at Poulton High School (not technically a High School, but so called) in Poulton-le-Fylde, just before her sixth birthday.

Her school reports reveal what became apparent in later life. Everything was "good", or "very good", or "excellent". She was deemed a most conscientious worker.

Her last term at the high school was a repeat of the previous terms – "good", "excellent".

She left with a glowing report to go to Lowther College, North Wales, where she blossomed. She was always the happiest of people, always the most popular.

On leaving Lowther, Valerie's bubbling restlessness and her flair for languages resulted in her becoming a travel representative for a firm called Gaytours. Now this was the 1950's, and Gaytours was what it said it was, a travel company.

You could have had a holiday in Majorca for thirty-three and a half guineas! Halycon days indeed!

She spent some time in Majorca, living with a resident travel representative, learning the travel business and about life.

The letters between her and my mother and father, whilst she was in Majorca, reveal a level of mutual adoration and love. By contrast, their letters to me in boarding school might as well have been written by robots.

Valerie was ambitious. She, my sister Marilyn, and a long time family friend, Peter, decided to form a trainee courier company, teaching young ladies to be travel couriers. At that time, to be a travel courier was not thought to be a suitable occupation for a young man.

In July 1964, after various classes near their office in Manchester, they arranged to take a party of trainees to Europe, to visit various hotels and to learn the job of being a courier on site, as it were.

So the stage was set for the final act in the tragedy of Valerie's life.

They hired a coach. There were thirteen young ladies, including my sisters, Peter and a driver. The momentum towards the final tragedy was inexorable.

Heading towards Lugano, Valerie having decided that she would describe the countryside, took up the microphone, and went to the front. She sat on the dashboard, with her back to the front windscreen, talking, joking and leading some singing.

Beloved Ghosts

The coach reached the top of the Biaschina hills, where there was a warning sign "Dangerous Bend & Steep Hill". Reaching the peak before the descent, the driver's foot slipped, and he lost control. It was quite clear that a major disaster was about to occur on the steep winding road, with the coach heading towards the edge, and the valley below.

As a last resort, the driver swung the wheel and turned the coach into a rocky retaining wall.

Luckily the wall just held, but the impact was such that it stopped the coach dead in its tracks, catapulting Valerie through the front window into the valley below.

She became the girl with the shattered face in my Guildford experience.

So there it was, everyone else survived, including my other sister Marilyn, who witnessed the accident. Valerie was in the wrong place, at the wrong time. In that moment of tragedy, the lives of my sister and my parents were changed forever.

My father telephoned me in the middle of the night to give me the news. He could not control his emotion and, at first, I could not really understand what he was saying.

When I had eventually worked it out, I immediately drove from my home to see my parents, and offer what comfort I could. I tried desperately to get news from Switzerland, hearing the sympathy of the continental telephone operators as they tried to make sense of what everybody was saying, offering me what comfort they could.

The following day I flew out to Milan, then took a train to Lugano.

I had the awesome responsibility of looking after eleven young ladies, my very distraught sister, a coach driver who was in bits and blaming himself for the tragedy, and the general manager, Peter.

By the time I had arrived, Valerie's metal coffin had already been sealed, which in many ways was a blessing.

I organised flights home for everybody, then flew home, taking Marilyn with me.

I arranged for a local firm of undertakers from home to meet the coffin at Heathrow airport. Peter very kindly agreed to travel with it as his last act of friendship.

Most of the daily papers carried reports of the crash and death.

Headlines from the papers read "Courier Girl Dies in Mountain Crash", "Flung From Coach, Courier Dies".

At the funeral, my father threw himself on the coffin and sobbed.

He, still badly affected by the war, deteriorated further from that moment on.

Ruth Dootson, Grandfather's Mother

1938 Wedding, Father and Mother

Father, Mother and Grandma Tay

Joseph (Father's Father), Mary (Father's Mother)

Ronnie (Mother's Brother) with Fiancée Irene

1937 Coronation Invitation

Grandmother, Lady Emery

Fat[her]

Gordon, Mother's Brother

Father standing by piano

1945 Election, Grandfather, Author, cousin Caroline, sister Valerie, Grandmother

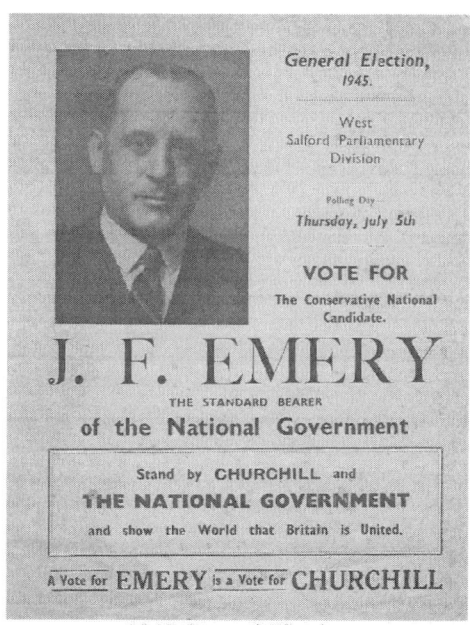

1945 General Election

Mother and Grandfather

Valerie, Mother, Marilyn

Beloved Ghosts

Gaytours Brochure, Valerie

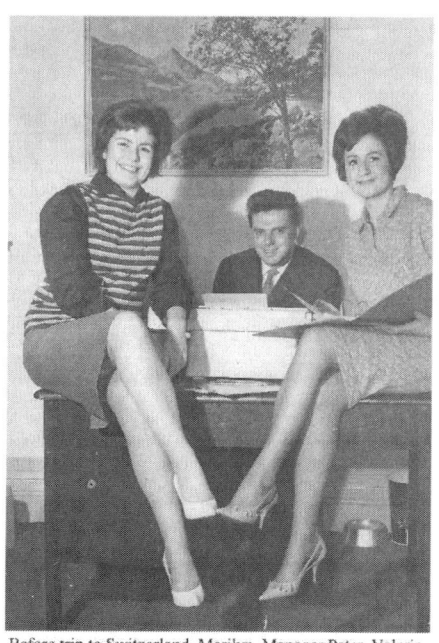

Before trip to Switzerland. Marilyn, Manager Peter, Valerie

Mother, Father, Grandfather, Auntie Amy

Dorothy

Tricia

Illawalla

Rock Garden, Illawalla

Vase hand painted by Deprez

Dining Room, Illawalla

Centre Hall, Illawalla, Grandfather, Valerie, Author, Marilyn, Mother

Illawalla Country Club Card

CHAPTER 12. A TERRIBLE INCIDENT – 1985

Fast forward from 1964 to 1985 – 21 years come and gone, a blur.
I have some memories of those years.
After qualifying as a solicitor in 1962, I continued to live in the Guildford area and commuted to Walton-on-Thames where I had my first employment as an Assistant Solicitor. I worked in a very small practice owned by a charming gentleman named Clifford Wells. He was anxious to retire and was desperately looking to sell out. Indeed, he was willing to almost give the practice away, virtually for nothing. I almost succumbed to the temptation to buy the practice, and started negotiating to buy a house (complete with tennis court) nearby. However, in the end, I succumbed to the pull of home, and decided that my future lay on the Fylde coast.

My mother sent me a cutting from a local newspaper with an advertisement for an assistant solicitor with W. Banks and Co, Solicitors in Blackpool.

I was very impressed when the principal of the firm flew down in his own plane to Guildford to interview me.

So, in 1963, I moved back north, and joined W Banks and Co. In 1964, I got married. Two eventful years!

W. Banks and Co was a lovely old fashioned firm, all the female staff were known as Miss or Mrs X, and the male counterparts were always Mr Y. No Christian names allowed! So it was always Miss Porter, Miss Middleditch, Mr Elston and Mr Baldwin.

As an assistant solicitor, I was expected to do everything. One had no need to specialise in those days. I would be in court in the morning, seeing somebody about a will at lunch time, and arranging for a house sale or a divorce in the afternoon.

The housing market was very sluggish at that time, and one or two conveyances per week was the norm.

In those distant days, the completion of a house sale and purchase was effected by the buyer's solicitor actually attending the office of the seller's solicitor to collect the title deeds and hand over a banker's draft, in return for which he or she was handed the title deeds to the property, and a Conveyance signed by the seller.

I had some enjoyable trips out of town to visit solicitors in far off mysterious places like Burnley or Bradford.

In 1967, my grandfather by then in his 80's, decided that he wanted to create a succession to the family cinema business, so he invited me to leave the law and run the family business in conjunction with my uncle, while he (my grandfather) retired.

I am sure this offer was made with the best of intentions, but there was little or nothing to do apart from collect rents and order confectionery for the sweet kiosks in each cinema. Grandfather, far from retiring, seemed to impose a stronger control upon the business in his declining years, although television and other entertainments, particularly bingo were reducing the faint grasp that cinema going had on the general public.

I occasionally took over as a relief manager for some of the cinemas. I found this a most enjoyable part of my job. Indeed on one occasion, I actually felt part of show business. The year was 1968. We had two Oscar winning films showing at two local cinemas at the same time – "Funny Girl" and "The Lion in Winter". It was a wet summer. Queues at the box offices. Grandfather said "It is just like the old days!", but of course it was not. How could it be, with the limited products from the studios, competition from TV and package holidays, cinemas sold for bingo or sold to operators who ran them into the ground?

I tried to expand and run some small businesses on my own.

For example, with a friend we developed one of the family properties, the Royal Pavilion Theatre in Blackpool.

The Royal Pavilion was Blackpool's oldest purpose built cinema but there was some doubt as to whether it was, actually, the first purpose built cinema in England.

Local Press ads for the opening in June 1909 included the line "Without a doubt, the finest and most up to date picture hall in England".

Beloved Ghosts

On July 27th 1917 the local paper, the Evening Gazette, featured an article by the newspaper's entertainment columnist E J Dromgoole. He wrote "There is no great and absorbing story concerning the Royal Pavilion in Rigby Road. Mr Alfred Blacker is the managing director of a small private company which runs the place as a picture pavilion. It was specially built for the purpose in 1909. Previous to that time, Mr Blacker had been presenting pictures at the Coliseum, but as that building was required for other purposes, the land in Rigby Road was purchased and in three months Mr Robert Fenton built the Royal Pavilion which opened on June 23rd 1909".

This article was written only eight years after the cinema opened and appeared to demonstrate that the Royal Pavillion was purpose built.

However, some people thought that the cinema was converted from a garage, and was not therefore purpose built. There is no conclusive proof either way.

When it opened it doubled as a theatre, and in the first year of opening, Charlie Chaplin is reputed to have appeared there as one of the Eight Lancashire Lads.

It closed during World War I and reopened in 1919. It was renamed the Futurist Cinema in 1929, and after World War II it was renamed the Alexander when Marks Cinemas of Manchester took it over.

Our family business, Fylde Cinemas Ltd took it over in 1948, and it reverted to theatre use. There was a weekly repertory company run by a lovely man named Jack Rose and it was also used by a local amateur repertory company, the Green Room Players.

Live theatre attendance declined along with cinema going, and the Royal Pavilion eventually became a strip tease theatre known as Arthur Fox Review Bar.

When his lease came up for renewal, Arthur Fox decided not to renew and the property became vacant.

My business partner and I decided to develop it, and it was converted into a licensed bar, betting shop, cafe and small cinema.

The licensed bar was known as Charlie's Bar in tribute to Charlie Chaplin.

I fulfilled a lifetime dream in the decoration and refurbishment of the bar.

It had a mini grand piano on a small dais in the centre of the licensed area. The pianist, resplendent in a dinner jacket was Jack Jumel, the brother of Betty Jumel of radio fame. Jack was also an accomplished player of the musical saw!!

The walls were decorated with original cinema posters from the Golden Age of Hollywood. It was beautiful.

However, in permitting myself the luxury of allowing my dreams to come true, I neglected to observe the simple fact that all businesses must make a profit.

The bar was packed every night with couples who would come in, sit down, order two halves of lager and spend the evening listening to the piano. A recipe for profit, it was not.

Obviously that could not continue, so we decided that a late license, and a bit more of a rowdy atmosphere would be more profitable, as indeed it was.

We provided different forms of entertainment, including one lady snake charmer, whose snake, true to expectations, escaped one night and caused havoc amongst the audience, which consisted of mainly young men who had come to look at the snake charmer rather than the snake.

The bar was trashed on a regular basis, but it was profitable!

Eventually we decided that the stress of providing entertainment each evening was too much and we sold out.

That was the final episode in my brief time out of the law.

Commerce was not for me and I decided that I needed the protection of the legal profession, where I was dealing with other people's money and not my own.

I joined a go ahead firm with offices in the Merseyside area, and I became based in their St Helens office.

My time in St Helens was happy for various reasons, and I want to say how straightforward and honest I found the people of St Helens to be. If one of them said that he or she would be in the office on Monday morning with whatever sum or document was required, he or she would inevitably turn up as promised.

I was never, to my knowledge, lied to and I found all my clients to be straightforward. The old, outdated, phrase "down to earth" springs to mind.

So, to revert to the saddest period in my life. On 22nd July, 1985, I was in my office in St. Helens. It seemed to be a normal day. Then, the police rang me. They checked that they were speaking to the person that they wanted to speak to, i.e. me, and they then said that there had been an incident at my parents' home, and that I should come back immediately. I remember saying to them "oh, has there been a burglary?" to which they replied "No, it's more serious than that, there has been an incident involving your mother."

I asked what incident it was, and I could hear a voice in the background saying "tell him the truth".

He spoke again "I'm afraid your mother is dead. Your father is with us and he is okay. Please come back as soon as possible."

I remember going into the secretarial room, feeling as if I was in a dream, to say that I had to go, as my mother had died.

You can imagine the looks on their faces at that news!

I then went into calm mode, giving instructions on what to do for various clients that day, just as if I was going to be back later on. Particularly, I remembered that there was money due back to Dorothy from the sale of her house.

My partner Graham came in and wanted to know what all the noise was about, and I told him. What could he say?

I then walked to the car park, exchanging pleasantries with someone along the way, and drove the fifty miles or so to my home at a normal speed. I can remember to this day that I talked to myself all the way saying that I had had a shock, and that I must be careful how I drove. I was also very measured in the calm conversation I had with some person on the way to the car park, whose name I cannot for the life of me now remember.

Before I left the office, I rang a former school friend of mine, a solicitor dealing in criminal matters in Blackpool, and asked him to look after father, which he did.

I went first to my own home to tell my wife what had happened. All she could say was "Has Mum gone then?"

I then went to my parent's house, which was heavily cordoned by police. I was met by a Chief Inspector, who told me that my father had battered my mother with a walking stick, and he had then gone to the garage and tried to kill himself, using the exhaust fume method.

As so often in his life, he failed even at that.

I then had the next task of telling my sister Marilyn, and for my own protection, as I did not know how she would react, I asked a policeman to go with me.

I went to her house. She came to the door and I told her exactly what had happened as there was no other way to do it. Her reaction was weird, she shrugged her shoulders as if she knew and said "it was bound to happen sometime".

I was so pleased that there had been no violent reaction, and took the opportunity to leave with the policeman without entering into any discussion.

The bad times with Marilyn were to come later.

I was in a ridiculously calm, automated frame of mind. I was ticking off in my own mind what I had to do as I knew that the occupancy of my parents' house had come to an end, and that father would never go back there again.

I know this is stupid, but I rang an Estate Agent and arranged for the house to be valued. I rang a jeweller to arrange for my mother's jewellery to be valued. I tried to ring the Rates department to explain the property would be unoccupied.

All within a few hours of my mother being killed. I was on autopilot, and in deep shock.

I rang my mother's best friend, Lillian. When she answered the phone she knew that, as I was ringing her, something had happened to my mother. "Is it Margie?" I said "Yes. He's killed her." I blurted out. I knew I was being brutal, but I did not know of any other way. I heard the phone being dropped at the other end, and then replaced.

That day, Blackpool South Shore Rotary Club was due to meet for its weekly lunchtime gathering. Father would have been attending as usual. I thought "well, he won't make that."

Beloved Ghosts

Ridiculous isn't it, the banal thoughts that go through one's head at a time of shock and crisis?

Apparently Lillian had rung her husband who had already left for the Rotary lunch, and I am told the meeting broke up in great confusion and sorrow.

I made sure the house was secure as best I could, put the burglar alarm on and went back to my own home. I cannot remember what I did or said, but I probably behaved as I normally did after a hard day at work. I know I was not in possession of any logical thought process. I was on automatic pilot, so I just watched television and tried to ignore the phone.

Eventually, I went to bed to be called at 3am by the Police. Would I please go to my parents' house as the burglar alarm was ringing and there had been an attempted break in?

Of course, the news had reached the papers and the evening edition of the local Gazette carried some of the story (as much as was known), from which the property could easily be identified.

On arriving at the house, I found that a brick had been thrown through one of the back windows, and that had caused the alarm to trip.

There were no other signs of a break in, and I was sure that my sister Marilyn was the perpetrator. She never admitted to actually throwing the brick, but she hinted at it several times in later life.

So that was the end of day one of my irrevocably changed life.

I went back to the house the following day. I was advised not to go to the bedroom where the event had occurred, my mother's body having been taken to the morgue. Apparently all the walls and ceiling were splattered with blood, and the Police did not think it appropriate that I should see that. I was grateful for their concern.

With the Police's permission, the room was cleaned, they having taken photographs of everything they wanted to see.

My solicitor friend saw my father through a brief court appearance, where he was remanded in custody.

Father did not want to see me because, as he told my solicitor, he thought that I would kill him in view of what he had done.

At the hearing, father was remanded to Risley Remand Centre, Warrington, for psychiatric examination, where I arranged to see him approximately two weeks later, after I had finally plucked up courage to agree to the appointment

In the meantime, I had to organise and endure mother's funeral.

I did not know how my sister Marilyn would react, so I arranged for two of my larger rugby playing friends to sit either side of her in case of emergency.

The service was conducted by a Rotarian Chaplain, an old friend of my parents, and was attended by hundreds of people.

I cannot remember what was said, or indeed, who spoke. I did not say anything.

The service and burial took place at Thornton Clevelys Parish Church, and mother was laid to rest next to her daughter Valerie (the same grave upon which father had flung himself, crying) and next to her father. She would have liked that.

Leaving the burial plot, I went back to the Church and saw a large number of people waiting for me to express their sympathy.

I could not face them, and just made a general announcement to all and sundry, thanking them for their attendance.

I now regret this and wish that I had spoken to everyone.

Life...regrets.

I then had to face the meeting with father at Risley Remand Centre. Can you imagine the conversation? Talk about an elephant in the room! He looked terrible. He had lost weight. His clothes were far too big for him, he could not sit still, and he continually brushed his hair back using the palms of both his hands. He was a wreck.

We talked about business, would you believe, because although I was now back in legal practice, he and I were still Directors of the family firm. We talked about rugby. We talked about generalities, my work, my children.

He seemed only vaguely aware of why he was where he was, but he did tell me that he felt safe there. There was no point in discussing what he had done, as nothing would change the facts, whatever his reasons or excuses for doing what he did. It was a case of going forward rather than looking back.

A few days later, he wrote to me, although the actual letter was written by a prison officer as he said he could not hold a pen.

In the letter, he was mainly concerned with material things, the furniture, the jewellery.

He was also concerned that Marilyn should be looked after.

I look at pictures of my mother. Who was this lady? A lovely person, I have no doubt. I remember her with the greatest love and affection, and will always do so.

Desperately torn all her life between looking after her father, my grandfather, and weighing that undoubted love for him against her duties as a wife of a most demanding, and probably mentally ill man.

No wonder she was torn apart. No wonder she suffered migraines. No wonder I often found her in tears, or in bed.

She once said to me that "If it weren't for you children, I would have left your father years ago."

As far as I was concerned, I wish she had. How different life would have been.

Life…choices…

Father remained on remand in Risley until the 10th September 1985 when he was granted bail on the condition that he reside at the Langdale Unit, Whittingham Hospital, Goosnargh under the care of Doctor Malcolm Burrell.

Whilst he was there he was medically examined as to his state of mind by Mr W K Lawson, the senior Medical Officer and visiting psychiatrist at Risley, and by Doctor Burrell.

I spoke with both men and found them to be professional, sympathetic, and in total agreement.

In his report, Doctor Lawson said that my father was very depressed, he had marked tremor in his hands, his concentration was poor and his attention span limited. He was aware of what he had done, but he could not elaborate on the circumstances.

On the 27th July 1985 while still in Risley, a serious psychotic episode had occurred, father visually hallucinating that he was seeing and describing objects that were not there. He became very aggressive and violent, and it was necessary to nurse him in an unfurnished room. He would not talk about what he had done, but he knew what he had done.

He subsequently became very paranoid, and complained that the staff were trying to poison him.

Although he was anxious to see me, he was so full of guilt that he believed that nobody would want to see him after what he had done.

He appeared to be suffering early stages of Parkinson's disease, although there was a slight improvement in his behaviour up to the time he was granted bail on condition that he resided at the Secure Unit at Whittingham Hospital, Preston.

His brain scans showed atrophy of certain areas of the brain, consistent with the normal process of ageing, but nothing more.

The report summarises father's life and confirms that over the years he consulted General Practitioners on and off for depression and insomnia. Indeed in 1975, he was considered to be suffering from endogenous depression and admitted to hospital for a course of ECT (Electroconvulsive therapy).

I remember collecting him from that appointment. I took home an almost speechless zombie, who took days to recover his "normality".

On the 26th May 1985, about two months prior to my mother's death, he had made a very determined attempt at suicide. He took an overdose of tablets he had hoarded over a period of time, and was in hospital for 48 hours in intensive care.

How much better for us all if he had never recovered.

Again, he refused to discuss the matter with me, my mother, or anyone in the family.

Doctor Lawson considered that father belonged to the "stiff upper lip" brigade, who feel in their heart of hearts that there is something improper about being mentally ill, and who attempt to solve their own problems, without talking the matter through at length with professional advisors.

His attempt at suicide, after he had killed my mother, was a very amateurish effort and, apparently, was very common where an elderly husband kills his wife.

Much of his unhappiness over the years may be attributed to the death of my sister Valerie, and the mental state of my other sister, Marilyn, together with the fact that as a result of his depressive illness, he felt that financial ruin was staring him in the face, and if he died, his wife would be left penniless.

Of course, nothing could be further from the truth. Mother was a wealthy lady in her own right.

It was the conclusion of both Medical Practitioners that at the material time father was suffering from an abnormality of mind, namely psychotic depression, such as would substantially impair his mental responsibility for his acts and omissions.

He was considered fit to plead guilty to manslaughter while the balance of his mind was disturbed.

He eventually went for trial on the 1st November 1985 pleading as advised.

Judge Sanderson Temple accepted father's plea.

This was part of his judgment.

"You left school, went into the printing business and you enlisted in the army during the war.

You became a Captain and served your country with distinction. You went into business when you came out of the army and embarked on a successful career. You became involved in civic affairs, became a councillor and a JP.

You did a lot of charitable work and during this time you had the confidence and support of a happy marriage and a loving wife.

That marriage survived great crises. At the end of seven decades mental enfeeblement led to delusions. You were subject to depression, and in the delusions you thought that after your death your wife would not be provided for.

It was then that you took her life."

Judge Temple made an order under the Mental Health Act that Father should be kept in a place of safety, Whittingham Hospital, until such time as he could safely be released under some form of supervision.

There then commenced a very difficult period in my life.

After a short time, most of father's friends abandoned him. My sister Marilyn visited him once, and indicated that she would never go again.

Father moved from Whittingham Hospital to a private nursing home near Ormskirk. I was living with my partner Dorothy nearby, and was able to visit him on a regular basis. I made every effort to be kind to him, but our conversations were, as always, stilted and unsatisfactory. He was a most resentful and embittered man. As far as he was concerned, he was not to blame for anything. Everyone else was at fault. He accused me of trying to rob him of his pension (not withstanding the fact of the fees in the nursing home exceeded his pension income by a considerable amount).

I left every meeting with a feeling of emptiness and guilt.

Someone once said that you can lose confidence only once. After that, it is gone forever. He or she was not necessarily right, as I was drained after every visit, losing my confidence over and over again.

He came to stay one night with Dorothy and I, and he spent the whole time pacing around, not sleeping. Of course, we had locked our bedroom door, out of fear, though neither of us would acknowledge that.

A couple of years after Dorothy died, I moved back to the Fylde Coast and I arranged for father to go into a nursing home in Blackpool and then one in St Annes. He had a period in the psychiatric unit at Victoria Hospital, Blackpool, where he refused to join in any form of group therapy, and generally made life as difficult as possible for me when I visited him.

After an argument one day, I told him that I was no longer scared of him and stormed out. That was not true. I would always be scared of him.

He was eventually moved to a private nursing home in the grounds of Whittingham Hospital where he died of emphysema (the same disease that had killed his father) in 1991.

I had had six years of visiting him almost weekly, and in those six years, he never expressed any gratitude or love for me.

He never apologised for what he had done, and never appeared to regret it.

Thinking about father one day, I suddenly realised that we had never really laughed together. He had a high pitched, nervous giggle. He never told jokes, and appeared not to understand them when he was told one.

Rather bizarrely though, I remember being with him in one of our family cinemas. The film was "Abbott and Costello meet the Keystone Kops".

There was a scene which involved mistaken identity. Father was doubled up with laughter, and in the end, I could not help myself, but join in. We laughed together for our one and only time.

His lecture on the facts of life was amusing, but only in retrospect. He waited until I was 17, by which time I knew more or less everything anyway.

He was quite succinct. "You know what happens, don't you? Well, don't do it until you're married, and women don't like it!".

What does that say about his relationship with my poor mother?

If ever there was a wasted life, it was his.

CHAPTER 13. DOROTHY – 1988

Let me tell you about Dorothy. Let me also tell you that she lived with me, and died with me.
She was an infant school teacher, only 9 months younger than me.
She came from a politically left family, but "left" in a way that I admired. They genuinely cared about other people, and society in general. They were not really interested in money or possessions, but provided more than the necessary material things for their family, as well as love and friendship.
Due to grandfather's influence, I had always been a right wing Tory, and had been brought up to beware of the Left. Dorothy's parents dispelled that worry, and I knew that if the majority of the people in their party were like them, there would be no fear for the future.
They were beautiful people, and I was very grateful to be part of their family. They had a genuine family life, unlike my own parents.
This will be one of the shortest chapters as there is nothing, yet everything to say about a short, loving, stress free relationship.
How can one describe happiness and then even more difficult, awful pain, except in a limited fashion, using the same old words.
In 1985, she walked into my office some weeks before my mother was killed.
She was divorced and buying a house.
We had a normal solicitor/client relationship until the traumatic event of my mother's death. After that, I needed comfort, and I am ashamed to say that I rejected comfort and love when it was offered to me by those closest to me at the time. My only excuse was that I was in such an emotional mess, totally devasted, that I sought comfort where perhaps, I should not have.
I have learned to live with that guilt, but it still haunts me.
Dorothy understood.
At that time, I was half living at home in Poulton-le-Fylde, but spending more time in St Helens, where I had my practice, staying in a house loaned to me by an Estate Agent friend.
There is little point in describing the pain of my subsequent divorce, and separation from my wife. She was in no way to blame, and any fault was mine and mine alone.
Those who have been through such proceedings will know, and do not need to be told. Those of you who have not, count yourselves lucky.
Eventually, Dorothy and I lived together, and were happy together. Her children were also happy for her, and they supported me in all sorts of ways. Like the rest of the family, they were kind and loving.
We bought a house.
In 1987, when we were on holiday in Cyprus, she started to suffer with a swollen stomach. She had a very heavy, painful period. On return from holiday, after an exploratory operation and after a visit to a specialist, following more x-rays and internal examinations, we were told she had ovarian cancer.
After a short stay in hospital, following the removal of the initial tumour, she came home. Then a terrible, but mercifully short, few weeks followed. It was a time of chemotherapy, bowel sectioning, weight loss. She moved downstairs to avoid having to climb the stairs, more time in bed, emaciated, more suffering.
There is no point in telling you any more. Those of you who have been through it will know of the stress.
Her parents were wonderful, caring as much for me as they did for Dorothy.
Midway through her treatment, a specialist assured us the cancer was fully cleared.
We laughed and cried.
We went to a nice hotel in Wales to celebrate.
We had a long weekend to remember, but even then, she was already becoming more tired.
On the Monday, she knew her cancer had returned. "The buggers back" she said.
From then on it was all downhill. A Macmillan nurse, a beautiful Irish lady, came to see out Dorothy's last few days with me.
She died on the 13th June 1988. She was 48. We were together two and a half years.
I was left on my own, in an empty house, playing the piano like Klipspringer.

Beloved Ghosts

    I stayed in the St Helens area for another two years or so, before returning to my roots on the Fylde coast. I opened an office in St Annes followed by another one in Blackpool...an endless progression of work. Looking back, I ask myself why. Escape?

    Dorothy is never out of my thoughts. Many years later, I wrote the following poem entitled "Summer" for and about her:-

Last summer, we watched some cricket,
And went for several walks.
We had lunch in a hotel,
And walked the grounds down to the beach,
Where the wind blew sand in our faces.
We watched a family at play,
Mother in charge, father complaining,
The two boys kicking a football.
We gardened a little, and then went to Italy,
Where we sat by the sea, and drank red wine,
Later in the year, we took a ship,
And sailed the Baltic.
The sun shone all day and it was nice to meet strangers.
When I say "we", I mean "me",
I was alone last summer.
You had died in another summer, years ago.

CHAPTER 14. MARILYN'S DISAPPEARANCE – 2001

My sister Marilyn was born in 1948. She was the apple of my father's eye and she was my sister Valerie's best friend.

She inherited father's nervous personality, and in many ways was a female replica of him.

He recognised that, so she was his favourite.

I was nine years older than her, and I thought of her as a mere girl. As a consequence, our paths seldom crossed after I brought her back from Italy following Valerie's death, which affected her very badly, and changed her character completely.

She became a chain smoker of such epic proportions, that the family were convinced that she suffered from severe nicotine poisoning.

Clearly her mental state was affected. She was subject to violent rages, and demanded attention whenever she sought it.

She could be physically violent and on one occasion, threw my mother bodily from her house.

All the family did its best to sympathise with her. We understood her feelings, but it was too difficult to make her see reason.

We were usually polite and indifferent to each other at joint family affairs, or during the holiday seasons.

Occasionally, I advised her on legal matters.

One year, she took a lease of a small kiosk on Blackpool South Pier, selling trinkets and miscellaneous rubbish, but that was an unsuccessful venture.

She also worked for me, in a secretarial capacity, for a time, but the strain of her proximity was too much for both of us, and she eventually secured a job with a local Building Society as a receptionist.

During that time I was working as a solicitor in Blackpool, and I last saw her in 2000, when she called into my office on some excuse. I asked my son Simon to sit in on the meeting, as, to tell the truth, I was rather scared of her and worried as to what she might do.

I last heard about her maybe a year or so later, when she rang from a hotel near where my sister Valerie had been killed. I received a call in my office, from a gentleman saying that he was the manager of the hotel, that my sister was staying with him, that she had lost her credit cards and had no money, and would I pay her bill?

I refused, and in case that sounds harsh, I would point out that my sister had all the monies from the sale of her house, and other substantial monies from my grandfather and my mother. She could easily have obtained a replacement credit card. She was just trying it on.

I have not heard from her, nor of her, from that day.

This is how she disappeared.

Early in 2001, I was in my office in Blackpool when I was told that there was a delivery for me. I went to reception and there was a courier with a trunk. He said it was from my sister, and that I should pay his bill.

I declined (politely), and asked him to take the trunk back to my sister, who at that time lived in Thornton Cleveleys.

He reluctantly did so, but about an hour or so later he was back again with the trunk, looking mystified.

Apparently, when he returned to my sister's house, it was deserted, without a stick of furniture in the property and no sign of any occupancy. So in the two hours that he was away, the house had been completely cleared and the estate agents "For Sale" sign removed.

I had no option, but to pay the courier.

In the trunk were various items of cosmetics, with a letter from Avon saying that my sisters' account was overdue, and demanding payment, and the other items as listed in her letter, including family photograph albums, in which I found pictures of my father had been stabbed through with a sharp implement, and his face obliterated.

Enclosed in the trunk was the following letter:

> Dear Dave,
> The contents of the trunk are of interest to you I'm sure. Take care of them.
> It may be a long time before we meet again so farewell brother, take care of yourself. I will send a postcard or two when I arrive at a settling place.
>
> Cordially,
Marilyn
>
> (Contents: books – records – photograph albums – tapestries – loose photos)

    My first thought was that she intended to kill herself, so I contacted the Police and asked if they could trace her.

    Within two days, they said they had found her, and that she was as well as could be expected, and that she did not want her whereabouts divulging.

    The Police could do no more as they had done their job in finding her.

    You will note that Marilyn addressed me as "Dave", just as the lady in Guildford had said.

    I then started to receive weird postcards from Torquay, Oxford, Paris, Portugal, and various other places, including Israel.

    Finally came the phone call from the hotel near Lugano and that was it.

    I have tried to trace her on several occasions through enquiry agents, but all they could tell me was that there was no record of her death in either the UK or Europe, and that she was not registered with any GP in the UK.

    So that is it, as far as I am concerned. I am fairly certain that had she been alive, and judging by her past performances, I would have heard from her if only by way of further adverse comment.

    Was the lady in Guildford correct? Had Marilyn gone over by her own hand? Did she not try to save herself? Or is she still alive somewhere? Maybe she will read this book? Perhaps she will get in touch? It would be nice to see her again.

CHAPTER 15. ANOTHER MEETING WITH FATHER – 2

There he was sitting in the sun. He looked as usual, a combination of angry and sheepish. We nodded to each other.
"Let's talk about you and what you did" I said.
"Why?" he replied "Why talk about it? It's done."
"It may be, but am I not entitled to know why?"
"It's alright for you."
"What do you mean it's alright for me?"
He shrugged, as if I should know what he was talking about.
"You wouldn't understand."
"Try me", I countered.
"You do not know what it was like. You have no idea, you had it so easy... Salford between the wars..."
And so he started to try and explain. This is a synopsis of what he said, I cannot convey the pauses, the shuffling, the stuttering, the looking away and the evasion.
"I was overwhelmed. We were not a rich family. My father was not a well man, suffering from emphysema all his life. He was a salesman, selling printing machinery. There was a depression and if it had not been for my mother he would not have survived. She encouraged him, cajoled him, threatened him and made him provide for us. Everywhere there was poverty. Meeting the Emery family, and particularly your mother, changed everything. The contrast between my home life and hers was stark..." and he rambled on, but I knew that what he was trying to tell me was that he was so far out of his depth in his relationship with my mother, and yet true to his personality, he was unable to confess or admit the error of his ways and his weakness.

He would say that he was being strong in sticking it out and keeping his promises, yet he just had to say "I am sorry, this is not for me. Please let me go." If he had, of course, then I would not be writing this, and much pain and sorrow would have been avoided.

So there we have it, was it backbone and guts that made my father persevere? Or was it weakness in him for failing to come out with the truth?

He just did not know how to cope with life.

It was all very well, closing one's public mind and face, and not talking about anything important, although never really shutting away the awful images of the walking stick, the bloodstained room, the solitary cell at Risley, the trial, and the long period of bitterness and resentment until his emphysema brought him to this place.

Punishment on earth? Does a person who is mentally ill, deserve punishment?

That is not for me to answer.

I got up, and walked away, leaving father sitting in the sun, outwardly calm, sun tanned, peaceful, but inwardly living a hell.

Beloved Ghosts

CHAPTER 16. TRICIA AND HER TRIP TO BRAZIL

I met Tricia on the QE2 in the early 1990's. She was travelling with her mother and lived on the Isle of Wight.

She (and her mother!) decided that we should be together, and so she came north, complete with two horses, a dog, a jeep, numerous books and her happy, joyous personality.

She found a job in a local school, and we bought a house in the Ribble Valley with sufficient land for her horses. I created a garden. After a few years, we moved to a bigger house, with a more beautiful garden, a stable and an arena.

We married. We socialised. We had a "normal" life. She rode her horses. I gardened and worked.

However, in 2002, after a routine mammogram, a lump in her breast was discovered. She had a lumpectomy and was given a five year course of Tamoxifen, which supposedly reduced the risk of any cancer returning.

Unfortunately, Tricia suffered serious side effects to the Tamoxifen, added to which she was also in the throes of an extreme menopause.

Her cancer eventually returned. She had a lumpectomy, then a mastectomy, followed by radiotherapy, then chemotherapy. All this was over a four year period, so by the time we got to early 2006, she knew that the prognosis was terminal.

She therefore looked for alternative avenues of healing. She changed to a natural health food diet. She met a faith healer in Clitheroe, who recommended as a last resort that she try John of God in Brazil.

Of course, I knew nothing about John of God. I was sceptical, as were all our friends. However, Tricia became convinced that this was the only way forward, and she asked if I would support her if she went to Brazil. She was clearly very ill and, despite my doubts, I had no choice.

What else could I do? In my heart, I knew she was dying.

I booked the flights and the cars, and Tricia made the necessary arrangements for her stay in Brazil.

It was essential that somebody accompanied Tricia as she was not well enough to look after herself. Her very good friend Maria, a horse enthusiast like Tricia, agreed to go with her. This was an unselfish gesture, as she was taking on a great responsibility.

Maria kept a diary of the visit, and I have left her actual words, as written, but where necessary I have inserted appropriate notes.

MARIA'S DIARY
Saturday 18th March
Boarded flight around 9:30 *(at Heathrow)* in evening but due to problems take off delayed until after 11, by the time we got to San Paolo Tricia exhausted so she was wheeled off in a chair, godsend really as delay had made us late for connection and we were whizzed through in plenty time. Brasilia flight awful we were so tired. Again taken off by wheelchair and put in a taxi. Didn't see much of anything then as both flat out until we arrived at Claudio and Miriam's *(C & M were their hosts for the visit. They were part of the resident organisation.)*
Sunday 19th March
Arrived about 2.30 after a gruelling 36 hour journey Just in time for lunch (in a communal canteen). People so friendly and welcoming. Already meeting people *(about ten in all)* who have had successful experiences so Trish hopeful and excited and looking forward to her "operation" on Wednesday. She is so exhausted so in bed straight after lunch and stayed there, eating her supper in bed. Accommodation very basic, metal beds with boards and a very thin mattress, together with a dresser and a fan and that was it. Did have a loo and shower though. Most worrying was the massive gaps under door and as it was straight onto the outside was very concerned about snakes. Ended up stuffing towels under the door every night!
Monday 20th March
Lovely sunny morning, Trish very perky after a good sleep. Met some Canadians Randy and Karen. She *(Karen)* had her op and was feeling hopeful, although she had an enormous tumour on the side

of her throat. This again gave Trish hope stayed at table for well over an hour and she *(Tricia)* had not coughed once. I went with Sebastian (a French guest) to the Casa *(the village and nerve centre)*, it was so peaceful. Tricia stayed in bed got up for dinner, but cough had returned so back to bed. *(When Tricia and Maria went to the Casa with Sebastian they saw shops selling things to help healing, lots of crystals set in sorts of jewellery, and large and small crystals to keep in the light for maximum healing. Apparently the crystals gave Tricia great faith and hope up to the moment of her passing. There was a pharmacy as well, where patients collected prescriptions for herbal tablets, which had been blessed by the entities, i.e. John of God's assistants.)*

Tuesday 21st March
Took Trish out in wheelchair to Casa *(about 15 minutes walk)*. She was feeling tight and coughing, but bright and cheerful, had a lovely few hours, saw so many exotic birds and eagles soaring over the valley. Such a hopeful place though the poverty in the village was heartbreaking. Went to introduction evening in readiness for tomorrow, but the same people asked the same questions over and over again, and drove us both mad. Got back and chatted to the others a time before bed.

Wednesday 22nd March
Just got off the biggest rollercoaster of emotion either of us have ever experienced. Arrived at Casa at 8am fortunately Randy offered to guide us and thankfully took control of the wheelchair. We witnessed an op where Joao removed a huge tumour from a man's head via his nose without anaesthesia he suffered no pain and little blood, afterwards he collapsed in a wheelchair. hearing such inspiring stories, can't help but be hopeful. Tricia had her op at 2pm. I had to wait outside. She had heat and stabbing pains all over her cancer area and was taken to a recovery room and then back to bed via Claudio's car. Before the op took place had to go to the current room where the vibrations from the monks humming were electric. We were handed a prayer within a leaflet of the Sacred Heart the print was tiny and though I yet again didn't have glasses could clearly read it, back to normal within an hour though. *(It appears that Tricia's 'operation' was merely a laying on of hands. The current room was almost like a church, with benches and men dressed in white sitting there. She assumed them to be monks or mediums, and they were producing the humming sound. The room was quite full, and they had to keep their eyes shut to meditate and pray. This room was attended by many people, tourists as well as the sick.)*

Thursday 23rd March
Trish in bed recovering has dizziness is very weak and shooting pains feels like she has electric shocks through cancer area, I can feel it myself when I put my hands on her. She is so frail but her spirit is strong, she has been talking about celebrating all the way home and drinking champagne.

Friday 24th March
A bad day so hot and airless she has problems with breathing. Sat outside for a couple of hours and again for an hour in the afternoon. Very worried she is getting weaker and stomach swelling have a feeling it has moved to her liver. Claudio says we should ask the entity if we should cut the visit short and go home next Friday, not telling Trish for fear she'll crash. He also says if her body is finished she will go to the spirit world.

Saturday 25th March
After a good night much better had tea in room and chatted as usual, then revved up the wheelchair and spent morning at the Casa bird spotting and reading. Trish walked more than she has. Sadly the night fever and stomach pains returned. Very thundery.

Sunday 26th March
Feeling better tightness gone and sore throat which has always been present gone. Went to Casa but then back to bed. Feverish. Karen continues to give us hope as her tumour shrinking and feeling much better. They go home tomorrow, she has a 9 year old son and is desperate to live. Amazing thunderstorm.

Beloved Ghosts

<u>Monday 27th March</u>
Bad day. Went to Casa in morning. Tricia so weak and faint. Back to bed. Randy and Karen left. Had photo shoot.

<u>Tuesday 28th March</u>
Went to Casa. So weak really struggling to stay in chair. Had to keep lying on benches, picked up sandwich from fruities bar, then back to bed. Brightened up by afternoon, had good dinner tonight, chicken salad and rice. Think we are both suffering from lack of food as so salty most is inedible. Played scrabble before bed. Lungs still more comfortable.

<u>Wednesday 29th March</u>
Went to Casa for revision. Tricia fainted when we got there and was taken to the infirmary where she stayed until revision. *(The revision consisted of queuing in the current room with Joao standing at the end to receive each person individually and bless them. He blessed Tricia, then someone wheeled her aside, and he held Maria's hands and told her that Tricia had an old soul that had lived many times, and that she was going to pass to the spirit world.)* Atmosphere electric. Got back for dinner, dreadful.

<u>Thursday 30th March</u>
Very unwell got runs and dizzy. I went to Casa and asked for continued healing and a safe journey home. Joao held my hand and said God will be with us had such a sincere face.

<u>Friday 31st March</u>
Leaving for Brasilia, Trish had a bad night tummy so swollen and is very weak even a loo trip is exhausting. Hotel in Brasilia fab, had lunch but called doctor as tummy is so hard and she is so unwell in bed. In hospital by 6.30 has partial blockage of intestines and infection, on drip.

<u>Saturday 1st April</u>
Bad night, was awake for most of it. Had tube inserted through nose to stomach, and had quite a bit of blood given. Still on intravenous antibiotics. Had 3 enemas. X-rays shows blockage clear.

<u>Sunday 2nd April</u>
Bad night due to back pain. Doctor still won't release us as potassium and albium levels low. After leaving hospital didn't write any more as poor Tricia was so desperately ill, took me all my time just looking after her. Eventually got her onto plane. Was touch and go whether they would let us onto flight home, told them Tricia had severe travel sickness but sure they didn't believe me. Think the only reason they let us on board we were first class and not in view of anyone else. The flight was a nightmare as poor Tricia was in such a state. Crew very kind to us.

****

End of Diary entries.

The limousine bringing Tricia and Maria back from Heathrow stopped at the front door of our house. Maria got out and said to me "I don't think that Tricia can walk, she will have to be carried. You will not recognise her. She is not the person who went away".

I asked the driver if he would help me carry Tricia, but Tricia must have heard this conversation. A steely look came over her face, and she got out of the car, a little frail thing, and forced herself to walk into the house and up the stairs to her bedroom, where she collapsed on her bed.

There was clearly no prospect of recovery. She deteriorated on a daily basis, and eventually went into Beardwood Hospital, Blackburn.

The care and love she received in Beardwood could not have been better, and I will be forever grateful to everybody there.

Maria stayed with her all the time, and I visited whenever I could.

At the beginning of her stay in hospital, and because she was pain controlled, she was convinced that she would be eventually coming home.

The most difficult day, was when the doctor had to tell her that she would never go home again, and that, in as many words, she would die in Beardwood.

The courage Tricia showed on that day far surpassed any bravery she had displayed in Brazil, and she became somehow at peace with herself.

It is clear that the whole Brazil experience gave Tricia great faith in the afterlife, and this enabled her to die with peace and dignity.

Shortly before she died, she and Maria were sitting on the side of her bed, looking out of the window. Maria asked her what she had seen, and she said "God, but I cannot go yet. David's not here".

The other day, I watched on YouTube a programme about what happened when people who had been terminally ill, died. The presenter spoke very eruditely about visions seen by the dying, angels, relatives, people sitting up at the last minute and talking. I knew he spoke sincerely, but it was not like that.

I was sitting with Tricia when she died. She did not sit up, she did not talk, there were no lights or shapes leaving her body. I just suddenly noticed that she had stopped breathing, and she had just slipped away.

Maybe like me, she had a near death experience, but it was just in her mind and she could not communicate it to anyone.

She was an extraordinary lady, and Maria was an extraordinary friend.

When Tricia first came to live with me from the Isle of Wight, she had clearly decided that she would not be leaving, and that her home would be permanently in the North. Early on in our relationship, she chose a green, natural, woodland burial site, adjacent to Clitheroe Cemetery. She also arranged for her coffin, whenever it was needed, to be made of wicker.

It was a grey, but fine day, at the burial site. No noise, apart from bird song.

There were a couple of readings, one by my daughter Pippa, in front of a silent, select group of friends and family.

We then went back to Chipping Parish Church for the service of celebration of Tricia's life. This was followed by a wake at the Gibbon Bridge Hotel in the Forest of Bowland.

In the order of service of celebration for the life of Tricia, and by way of tribute to Maria, I printed the following poem:

"For Tricia's love of horses – "A Blessing" by James Wright 1927-1980
Just off the highway to Rochester, Minnesota,
Twilight bounds softly forth on the grass.
And the eyes of those two Indian ponies
Darken with kindness.
They have come gladly out of the willows
To welcome my friend and me.
We step over the barbed wire into the pasture
Where they have been grazing all day, alone.
They ripple tensely, they can hardly contain their
Happiness that we have come.
They bow shyly as wet swans. They love each other.
There is no loneliness like theirs.
At home once more, they begin munching the young tufts
Of spring in the darkness.
I would like to hold the slender one in my arms,
For she has walked over to me and nuzzled my left hand.
She is black and white, her mane falls wild on her forehead,
And the light breeze moves me to caress her long ear
That is delicate as the skin over a girl's wrist.
Suddenly I realise
That if I stepped out of my body, I would break into blossom."

Following the wake, I was driven to our home, which had been empty, apart from me, for a long time, so nothing seemed any different.

Clothes, books, belongings, the Will – all to sort out, all would wait their due turn in the fullness of

Beloved Ghosts

time.

Joao Teixiera de Faria, known also as Joao de Deus, was a Brazilian medium and "psychic surgeon". He was based in Abadiania, Brazil, where he ran the Casa de Dom Inacio de Loyola, a "spiritual healing centre".

I do not propose to repeat here all the information about Joao that can be readily obtained online, nor to comment on the fact that in 2018 he became a subject of what prosecutors consider potentially the largest sexual abuse scandal in Brazil.

In December 2019, he was sentenced to 19 years and 4 months for the rapes of four women. In January 2020, he was sentenced to an additional 40 years for five further offence of rape.

To balance it up, there are also reports of his successful healings and the investigations into his "treatments" which partly exonerated him.

Who knows what the truth of it all is? Maybe it will come out eventually, but how will that affect the many people who considered they were 'cured' by him?

That was dear Tricia's sad story.

I remained in our house for another 3 years, but my heart had gone out of it, and the garden. I eventually sold, to go first into a rented property and then eventually purchased a property in Goosnargh, where I lived for 12 years. I was in a community of about five houses, in the countryside, with lovely neighbours and I achieved a certain calm and happiness.

CHAPTER 17. EPILOGUE

So that is it, a part story of my life – the coming to terms with certain things.

It must have seemed from the preceding chapters, that I had spent my life in mourning, and all my time attending funerals or cremations.

Nothing could be further from the truth.

I reflect on my life and consider that it has, in the main, been happy. Indeed, some events and times have been stunningly happy, maybe to compensate for the bad times, which I have undoubtedly suffered.

Take my piano playing for example. I was never as good a player as father, but nevertheless reasonably competent.

I played at parties, whenever there was a piano.

One year, on a rugby trip to London, my friend Rodney and I ended up in a piano bar in the West End.

The place was packed, people dining and drinking…but no piano music! Apparently the pianist was ill, so I asked the manager if I could play quietly in the background.

He was happy for me to do so, so I sat down to play. I was sure that I could not be heard above the general level of conversation, the clinking of glasses, and laughter. However, I gradually became aware that people were actually listening to me. I even received one or two rounds of applause. A gentleman came over to me, stuck a £5 note in my top pocket and asked me to play "Embraceable You". It was like a TV advert, 'everybody was amazed when he got up to play'. In that one night, a life time fantasy came true.

On another similar occasion, I was on holiday at the Burgh Island Hotel, where I played the piano on Christmas Eve.

A lady rested her chest on my shoulder, and said <u>please</u> play something by Cole Porter. Her musical knowledge must have been somewhat limited, as I was playing 'Night and Day' at the time!

Famous past guests at the hotel included Edward VIII and Mrs Simpson and, my particular hero, Noel Coward. I do not know whether I was playing on the actual piano used by him, but I like to think that I was.

Happiness comes in many guises, and I feel that I was blessed with very many occasions of happiness, notwithstanding the tragedies.

I spent a lot of time laughing.

I cannot say that I was particularly enamoured with my legal career however, which was nothing to speak of.

It fulfilled a need in terms of providing the necessary income for me to live and support my family. It provided good exercise for my heart, in that it was continually jumping into my mouth, and then back to a resting position in my chest. I felt at times owned by my clients, and by my staff who, nevertheless, were mostly good to me and worked hard. In return, I tried to treat them decently, providing sympathy at times of distress, and bonuses whenever I could.

As the property market expanded, we expanded, and as the property market crashed, so did we – not in bankruptcy or liquidation terms, but just a gradual diminishing of business, a raft of redundancies, and eventual closure of the office, for me to become a consultant for a large firm, working from home, with no staff or other responsibilities, except to the clients I took with me.

This instant reality firm was based in Guildford! Talk about life going full circle.

I became a part time Deputy District Judge, sitting in Preston, Acrington, Blackburn, Chorley and other points North.

I found the work interesting, but it was difficult to take time out from the office when the practice was so busy.

Overall, the law and I were not that compatible. I think I was competent, and I worked as hard as I could to build up the practice and the trust of my clients. It was a safe financial haven, and I stuck it out. I only retired when I was 78, having been qualified for 56 years.

One of the biggest joys of my life was sport.

I played club tennis in the summer, as well as going on an annual cricket tour to Sussex with a school old boys' side, but my main sport was Rugby Union (although I liked Rugby League as well).

Beloved Ghosts

I was selected to play for England Schools in 1956 and 1957. The 1956 side contained Richard Sharp, the future outstanding England fly half.

I joined Fylde Rugby Club just before I left school, playing in the schoolboy trials. When I walked to the ground for the first time, over the bridge, down Woodlands Road, in Lytham St Annes. I never realised how much that rugby club would become part of my life, and how important it would be to me.

Fylde was not one of the top Rugby Clubs. There were no leagues when I started playing, but the Daily Telegraph ran what was called the Northern Merit Table, in which Fylde featured. We had a strong fixture list. Every week international rugby players would be appearing for the opposition. We had our share of stars as well, including Malcolm Phillips, the England centre, and Mike Hindle, an outstanding Lancashire prop.

We had fixtures against Wasps, Leicester, Saracens, Coventry, Gloucester, Bristol and Sale, amongst others, as well as playing strong Welsh clubs, Aberavon and Llanelli.

Although we trained hard in those days, there was none of today's professionalism. Whilst winning was important, having a good time was equally so.

The best thing about Fylde was its inclusivity. It was, with the local Cricket Club, the social centre of Lytham in the late 50's/early 60's. The club was well supported, and the social events were sold out. It was the early days of the Beatles and the Saturday night dances were fronted by a group called Bobby Kingston and the Dynamites. We jived in our 60's gear, thinking how magnificent we all were...such fun, such happiness.

Walking into the club house after a game, into the noise and hubbub of the crowded bar, greeting friends, having a drink, was just the best feeling.

I was Captain of the club for a season. I played for Lancashire, and went on tour to Canada and East Africa with the Anti-Assassins.

I could, of course, tell you rugby stories that would make you sit up and take notice, but, what happened in the past, stays in the past, and I am so lucky to have such memories.

I paid a price for my love of sport however, suffering seven (yes, seven), hip replacement operations.

So, I am nearly at the end. I have deliberately not mentioned my lovely children, but only out of respect for their privacy.

They have been wonderful to me, kind, loving and helpful.

I know I can turn to them in any emergency, or for help with any problem.

I am also proud to have three grandchildren, and three great grandchildren.

So you see, it all balances up at the end, deaths for happiness. Is that a fair trade off? Who knows, but it does not matter what I think, because this has been my life, and I have lived it as I thought fit, at the time, complete with a multitude of mistakes.

CHAPTER 18. FINAL MEETING WITH FATHER – 3

"Hello…" I thought, "what's wrong?"
Father was coming towards me, and he was smiling!
"Ah" I thought, "he is going to say something bad to me, or about me."
I braced myself.
"I have a surprise for you" he said, not even through gritted teeth.
"For me?"
"I thought you might like to see some of your old friends."
"But why? You never liked them."
Was this a mystery? Perhaps father had actually approved of some of my friends.
"Come with me" he said, "you will see"
Who was this man? Why was he being nice to me?
Perhaps I had failed at something, because he always found it easier to be kinder to me under the shadow of failure, rather than in the gloat and glare of triumph. I cannot claim that that was an original thought, as that is what Dr. Waugh said about his son Arthur, who, in turn, was the father of Evelyn and Alec.
He took my arm. I recoiled, as he had recoiled from me so many times in his life. He shrugged, and limped off into the distance. I followed him, intrigued and apprehensive at the same time.
Eventually we came to an old theatre. I think it was owned by the family many years ago, now dilapidated.
There was a stage however, a few seats, and because we were in an afterlife, the footlights all worked, and by a miracle, so did the curtains.
We sat down.
Overture. Beginners. A blast of brassy music from a non-existent pit orchestra.
Chorus girls, tall in tights, high heels, strutting their stuff to the music.
A set of stairs suddenly materialised. Down the steps came the girls, one by one, but on each arm there were other people, male or female, elegantly dressed, also dancing to the music as best they could, trying to keep pace with the girls.
They were old and young. Sometimes the same person I had known in my youth, and later an older version of the same person. Some had aged well. Some not.
All had passed on, because do not forget – we were in another place, not necessarily heaven, but we were definitely somewhere.
I am not sure whether they saw us, or could even see anyone or anything. They all had smiles on their faces and (was I deluding myself?) their smiles seemed genuine.
Some people I did not know, but then I realised they were the older versions of my school friends and the friends of my adolescence.
My best friend from school, John B, had become rather large and had lost all his hair. I remember as a schoolboy visiting him at his home. His mother had bought a special chip pan, as she had been told I liked chips. Did I? I cannot remember.
Other friends from school followed, friends from my youth, friends from my middle age, just friends.
How effective my father had been, if, indeed, he had chosen the people I had viewed, but how had he known? How had he done it?
Random thoughts, but then I realised, all this was a fantasy. Idle longings, yearning for the past. Remember, I said at the beginning that we all live in a cocoon of memories, and here they are, the memories, I mean.
All the visions or mirages were accompanied by music, "my music" I like to call it. My friends thought I had peculiar musical taste. I agree. I am sure it was the frustrated hoofer in me, so the swing bands and vocalists of the 30's and 40's were always my choice. Probably that love of music was one of the few things my father gave to me, because, of course, he was brought up in that era.
So my music, and my memories, and my friends (no enemies) were all combined in this one last gift from father.

Beloved Ghosts

"Let's keep on dancing, let's keep on dancing, do not let the magic disappear".

On and on went the parade, the girls from the Town Hall, Cyril and Ronnie, dear Rex, Rodney a friend for all time, my sister Valerie, miraculously repaired, with her famous smile, equally repaired mother, and Dorothy, smiling and waving – acknowledging but saying nothing, disappearing before they went into the wings.

In the background, always the sound of laughter pouring from the rafters. An overwhelming sense of happiness and joy.

Friends. Friends. Adolescent friends. Old friends. I have just had the thought that while I can see all these people, you cannot know them. I thought I would have to paint a picture of each of them for you... but I cannot, as that would be too overwhelming and too emotional. So just imagine the people in *your* life, the people who made *you* happy, parading in front of you for one last time, moving to the music you loved. Smile at them, blow kisses to them, wave them off the stage into your past, never to be forgotten. They would always be playing *your* song.

This is a book of hope.

We are sustained by music and memories, and kindness, and laughter.

Remember these are the best of times.

In that moment, I became reconciled with father. We shook hands, and went our separate ways.

I finally understood that father, through no fault of his own, had been doomed from the start and then damaged beyond recovery. My mother and I were just two more casualties of war.

Beloved Ghosts

I would like to thank John Muter, David Maudsley, John Fryer, Sally Banister, Sharon O'Gara, Stephen and Caroline Boyle, and especially Maria Stevenson, Barry Band, and Christine Storey for all their helpful comments and advice.

David Taylor is a retired solicitor.

Beloved Ghosts

Printed in Great Britain
by Amazon